THE IMPORTANCE OF

Frank Sinatra

These and other titles are included in The Importance Of biography series:

Maya Angelou
Louis Armstrong
James Baldwin
The Beatles
Alexander Graham Bell
Napoleon Bonaparte
Julius Caesar
Rachel Carson
Charlie Chaplin
Charlemagne
Winston Churchill
Christopher Columbus
James Dean
Charles Dickens
Emily Dickinson
Walt Disney
F. Scott Fitzgerald
Anne Frank
Benjamin Franklin
Mohandas Gandhi
John Glenn
Jane Goodall
Martha Graham
Lorraine Hansberry
Stephen Hawking
Ernest Hemingway
Adolf Hitler
Harry Houdini

Thomas Jefferson
John F. Kennedy
Martin Luther King Jr.
Joe Louis
Douglas MacArthur
Thurgood Marshall
Margaret Mead
Golda Meir
Mother Jones
Mother Teresa
John Muir
Richard M. Nixon
Pablo Picasso
Elvis Presley
Eleanor Roosevelt
Margaret Sanger
Oskar Schindler
Dr. Seuss
Frank Sinatra
William Shakespeare
Tecumseh
Jim Thorpe
Queen Elizabeth I
Queen Victoria
Pancho Villa
Leonardo da Vinci
Simon Weisenthal

Frank Sinatra

by Adam Woog

Lucent Books, P.O. Box 289011, San Diego, CA 92198-9011

Library of Congress Cataloging-in-Publication Data

Woog, Adam, 1953–
  Frank Sinatra / by Adam Woog.
      p. cm. — (The importance of)
Includes bibliographical references and index.
Summary: Profiles the life and work of Frank Sinatra including:
growing up in Hoboken, life on the road, the classic years, and
the last decades.
  ISBN 1-56006-749-7
  1. Sinatra, Frank, 1915—Juvenile literature. 2. Singers—
United States—Biography—Juvenile literature. [1. Sinatra,
Frank, 1915– 2. Entertainers. 3. Singers.] I. Title. II. Series.
  ML3930.S56 W66 2001
  782.42164'092—dc21

                                                    00-009902

Contents

Foreword

THE IMPORTANCE OF biography series deals with individuals who have made a unique contribution to history. The editors of the series have deliberately chosen to cast a wide net and include people from all fields of endeavor. Individuals from politics, music, art, literature, philosophy, science, sports, and religion are all represented. In addition, the editors did not restrict the series to individuals whose accomplishments have helped change the course of history. Of necessity, this criterion would have eliminated many whose contribution was great, though limited. Charles Darwin, for example, was responsible for radically altering the scientific view of the natural history of the world. His achievements continue to impact the study of science today. Others, such as Chief Joseph of the Nez Percé, played a pivotal role in the history of their own people. While Joseph's influence does not extend much beyond the Nez Percé, his nonviolent resistance to white expansion and his continuing role in protecting his tribe and his homeland remain an inspiration to all.

These biographies are more than factual chronicles. Each volume attempts to emphasize an individual's contributions both in his or her own time and for posterity. For example, the voyages of Christopher Columbus opened the way to European colonization of the New World. Unquestionably, his encounter with the New World brought monumental changes to both Europe and the Americas in his day. Today, however, the broader impact of Columbus's voyages is being critically scrutinized. *Christopher Columbus,* as well as every biography in The Importance Of series, includes and evaluates the most recent scholarship available on each subject.

Each author includes a wide variety of primary and secondary source quotations to document and substantiate his or her work. All quotes are footnoted to show readers exactly how and where biographers derive their information, as well as provide stepping stones to further research. These quotations enliven the text by giving readers eyewitness views of the life and times of each individual covered in The Importance Of series.

Finally, each volume is enhanced by photographs, bibliographies, chronologies, and comprehensive indexes. For both the casual reader and the student engaged in research, The Importance Of biographies will be a fascinating adventure into the lives of people who have helped shape humanity's past and present, and who will continue to shape its future.

IMPORTANT DATES IN THE LIFE OF FRANK SINATRA

1915
Frank Sinatra born in Hoboken, New Jersey, on December 12.

1939
Marries Nancy Barbato; joins Harry James Orchestra.

1940
Joins Tommy Dorsey Orchestra; first child, Nancy, is born.

1951
Divorce Nancy Sinatra and marries Ava Gardner

1935
Wins *Major Bowes' Original Amateur Hour* radio talent show as a member of the Hoboken Four.

1946
Meets Ava Gardner.

1910	1915	1920	1925	1930	1935	1940	1945	1950

1938
Finds first regular singing engagement, as a singing waiter at the Rustic Cabin.

1942
New Year's Eve concert at New York's Paramount Theater causes pandemonium. Makes first recordings under his own name; quits Dorsey to go solo.

1948
Third child, Christina, born.

1944
Second child, Frank Jr., is born.

1941
Voted best male vocalist in *Billboard* and *Down Beat* magazine polls.

1943
Appears in first starring movie role, *Higher and Higher.*

1953
Signs with Capitol Records; makes the first of his classic albums with arranger Nelson Riddle.

1960
Makes first Rat Pack movie, *Ocean's 11*; forms own record label, Reprise.

1966
Marries Mia Farrow.

1976
Marries Barbara Marx.

1995
Sells Rancho Mirage compound; makes last public singing appearance.

1993
Duets, first recording in a decade, released to great popular acclaim.

| 1955 | 1960 | 1965 | 1970 | 1975 | 1980 | 1985 | 1990 | 1995 |

1971
Announces retirement.

1973
Ends retirement.

1998
Dies in Los Angeles on May 14.

1954
Wins Oscar for his supporting role in *From Here to Eternity*.

1988
Reunites members of the Rat Pack for a tour.

1981
Produces and directs President Ronald Reagan's inaugural gala.

1985
Receives Presidential Medal of Freedom, one of many such honors.

The Voice

There are endless stories about the tantrums, the bad behavior, and the gangster friends; and a billion words have been written about the music. But you can't have one Sinatra without the other.

—biographer Donald Clarke

Frank Sinatra—the Voice, Ol' Blue Eyes, the Chairman of the Board—was many things.

Above all, he was, in the opinion of many, the greatest single pop singer of the twentieth century—the premiere interpreter of what is generally called the Great American Songbook. This rich body of song, created during (but not limited to) the peak years of the Broadway musical in the 1930s, '40s, and '50s, encompasses the work of such gifted composers as Cole Porter, Jerome Kern, Richard Rodgers and Lorenz Hart, Johnny Mercer, Jule Styne, Harold Arlen, and George and Ira Gershwin.

This period is often described as the golden age of songwriting, the Renaissance of American music. At their best, the songs from this era were complex, multilayered in meaning, intensely emotional, and inventive in their melodies.

Often called standards (because they have become standard items in the repertoire of jazz musicians and pop/jazz singers), they were a marked change from the disposable melodies and lockstep rhythms of Tin Pan Alley that came before them; they differed as well from the high decibel, backbeat sounds of rock that came later.

Sinatra stood at a crucial midpoint in American music; his singing, characterized by both sensitive emotional power and freewheeling swing, bridges the gap between the nonswinging, carefully composed pop of the early twentieth century and the wilder freedoms that rock later brought in. Although the styles have obvious differences, Frank Sinatra's music was, in a very real way, a precursor to the best rock and roll. It had, and still has, the same immediacy, the same idiosyncrasy, and the same naturalness of expression. Bono, from the band U2, touched on another aspect of Sinatra's appeal to rockers—his self-confident, virile persona—when he presented the older singer with a Lifetime Achievement Grammy Award in 1994: "Rock-and-roll people love Frank Sinatra," Bono remarked, "because Frank Sinatra has got what we want—swagger and attitude."[1]

ACHIEVEMENTS

Dozens of singers have made the Great American Songbook their special province; Billie Holiday, Sarah Vaughan, Ella Fitzgerald, Johnny Hartman, Rosemary Clooney, and Tony Bennett are only a few of the best known. No one, however, has ever sung them with more confidence, emotion, and style than Frank Sinatra.

Sinatra certainly recorded his share of poor-quality music. But the best of it—created with such superb collaborators as Tommy Dorsey, Axel Stordahl, Nelson Riddle, Billy May, Jule Styne, and Jimmy Van Heusen—has a timeless quality that transcends generations.

Faultless diction, liquid phrasing, perfect timing and pitch—all contributed to Sinatra's unmistakable sound. Adding to these was the conviction of his singing; he sang every word as if he really meant it, and the emotional depth he conveyed to his audiences was unlike anything anyone had ever heard before. Sinatra *believed* what he sang, and his fans believed him.

As an artist, Sinatra was also remarkably long-lived: He sustained his career, at the highest level possible, longer than perhaps any other single figure in popular music. He became rich and famous at an early age, and although he nearly destroyed his career at one point, a dramatic comeback made him an even greater celebrity and artist than before.

Another of Sinatra's notable achievements was not strictly musical; it was, instead, a triumph of the American dream. Sinatra's life embodied a classic story: the son of immigrants, a product of the urban Northeast, finds immense success, wealth, and fame through talent and hard work. At the same time, the singer was a lifelong champion of equality among races and ethnic groups, and, in the opinion of journalist Pete Hamill, this attitude ultimately affected his music:

Many people consider Frank Sinatra the greatest pop singer of the twentieth century.

Sinatra created something that was not there before he arrived: an urban American voice. It was the voice of the sons of the immigrants in northern cities—not simply the Italian Americans, but the children of all those immigrants who had arrived on the great tide at the turn of the century. . . . Frank Sinatra was the voice of the twentieth-century American city.[2]

INFLUENCE AND INNOVATION

Like any musician, Sinatra was influenced by others; singers like Louis Armstrong, Billie Holiday, and Mabel Mercer left their mark on his style, and he also learned a great deal from musicians like bandleader Tommy Dorsey.

The most important of these tutors was Bing Crosby. When Sinatra was an aspiring singer, Crosby was the most important and famous pop performer in the world. For decades Crosby's easygoing personal style and soothing voice had a profound influence on the direction of American pop music, and Sinatra listened carefully. But the younger man took Crosby's approach a step further; as music critic Whitney Balliett notes, "His voice was smaller and lighter than Crosby's, but his phrasing and immaculate sense of timing gave it a poise and stature Crosby's lacked."[3]

Sinatra was never, strictly speaking, a jazz singer. He never improvised and rarely "scatted" (that is, used nonsense syllables to imitate an instrument), these being two hallmarks of the pure jazz singer. Sinatra was, instead, a classic pop singer, though one who was deeply influenced by jazz. Critics have detected other influences as well, notably the style of traditional Italian singing known as *bel canto*. For his part, Sinatra always referred to himself simply as "a saloon singer."

Sinatra's voice was a marvel by itself, but behind it was much more. He found many ways to innovate. For one thing, he had a shrewd ability to adapt to new technology as it developed. He was able to exploit the still relatively new phenomenon of radio to extend his own fame, and he used the long-playing record album to explore the artistic possibilities of recording technology.

Sinatra was deeply influenced by the musical style of Bing Crosby (pictured).

ALL THAT TRULY MATTERS

Journalist Pete Hamill, in this excerpt from his book Why Sinatra Matters, *reflects on what Sinatra meant to him.*

"I liked his doubt and his uncertainty. He had enriched my life with his music since I was a boy. He had confronted bigotry and changed the way many people thought about the children of immigrants. He had made many of us wiser about love and human loneliness. And he was still trying to understand what it was all about. His imperfections were upsetting. His cruelties were unforgivable. But Frank Sinatra was a genuine artist, and his work will endure as long as men and women can hear, and ponder, and feel. In the end, that's all that truly matters."

More significantly, Sinatra was the first singer to fully exploit another technological innovation, the microphone, using it to extend his voice intimately and evocatively to his audiences. Sinatra's canny use of the microphone played no small role in the phenomenon known as "Swoonatra"—the hordes of screaming young women who thronged to his shows in the 1940s.

His career as a movie actor was less innovative, but Sinatra was able to sustain it for decades. Many critics feel that Sinatra's abilities as an actor were never fully utilized; his movies are uneven in quality, but the best of them—notably *On the Town* and *From Here to Eternity*—remain classics.

A COMPLEX MAN

But Sinatra was not just a brilliant performer. For almost his entire adult life, he was also a world-famous celebrity with a messy personal life, powerful friends, and a complex, often erratic personality.

On the one hand, Sinatra could be a boor. He often displayed a disagreeable temper and exhibited thuggish behavior. He was a terrible husband and an inadequate (if loving) father. If he felt a friend had insulted or betrayed him, he was quick to drop that friend from his world. The innumerable stories of his swiftness to fight (or to direct an associate to do the brawling for him) are further indications of deep-seated character flaws.

On the other hand, Sinatra could be expansively generous and considerate. He could be a charming and witty companion if he wanted to. He loved to give expensive gifts, and he was constantly taking on the problems of friends (or even strangers) as if they were his own. He quietly picked up medical bills for friends in need, and he raised millions of dollars for charities. He was especially courteous to

Sinatra achieved unparalleled success and wealth, but his personal life was often chaotic.

women, forbidding anyone to use coarse language around them and carefully catering to their needs. He was so solicitous of guests at his house that friends called him "the Innkeeper."

He had many friends, too, from a wide range of callings: entertainment figures, gangsters, musicians, casino owners, politicians. Sinatra's associations with gangsters would dog him all his life, and his friendships with politicians would be the source of both great joy and great disappointment.

Sinatra loved gambling, whiskey and cigarettes, and the company of glamorous women; his reputation as a Casanova was unparalleled during his day. A chronic insomniac, he generally stayed up all night, restlessly moving from one place to another, and catnapped during the day. He often described himself as "a fourteen-karat manic-depressive," adding that this gave him experience with both the heights and the depths of emotion.

"THE SAME GUY"

Adding to this complex set of characteristics was a reputation for complete and absolute honesty, for always saying exactly what was on his mind even if his words were painful. A longtime friend, actor Cary Grant, once remarked, "Frank is a unique man. Utterly without hypocrisy, bluntly yet loyally opinionated. . . . It's almost frightening to some, to be faced with honesty."[4]

All of which creates an intriguing enigma for Sinatra fans and foes alike. Onstage, he was capable of the subtlest nuances of romantic expression; offstage, he could be brutal, crude, and controlling. He was outspoken about his liberal and tolerant views at a time when few entertainers announced their political feelings, and he stubbornly clung to those views during dangerous times of intolerance; but he was also capable of making coarse ethnic jokes in public and in private, and he adopted politically conservative viewpoints late in life. Onstage and on record, he was a soulful loner; in private life, he craved nonstop action and the constant attention of friends and associates.

In the end, according to biographer Donald Clarke, it is necessary to understand and accept both the light and the dark sides of Sinatra's personality and music. Clarke writes:

> There has been a lot of reporting about his bad behavior and, separately, millions of words about his music. In a curious way we have taken the two Sinatras for granted. Yet he became perhaps the most famous man of the century because the great singer and the troublemaker were in fact the same guy.[5]

The solution to this enigma remains tantalizingly elusive. Some clues, however, may be found in Sinatra's hometown of Hoboken, New Jersey.

1 Escaping Hoboken

To get to the bustle of Manhattan from Hoboken, New Jersey . . . takes about fifteen minutes by ferry; to forget the deadliness of the place took Frank Sinatra most of his lifetime.

—biographer John Lahr

During the great wave of immigration to America between 1876 and 1914, millions of people arrived hoping to find a better life than the poverty-stricken ones they had left behind. Among them were Frank Sinatra's parents, then two young children from Italy. Their respective families both settled in Hoboken, New Jersey, across the Hudson River from Manhattan.

Anthony Martin Sinestro, called Marty, was from Sicily; Natalia della Garavanti, nicknamed Dolly, came from Genoa. They met as teenagers, began courting, and were married on Valentine's Day 1914. The couple settled in a small cold-water flat at 415 Monroe Street in Hoboken, where, on December 12, 1915, Dolly gave birth to a son.

The baby weighed over thirteen pounds at birth, and the delivery was so difficult for the diminutive Dolly that it left her unable to have more children. The doctor had to use forceps during the birth, which scarred the baby's cheek and neck and punctured an eardrum. It was such a difficult delivery, in fact, that according to Sinatra family legend the doctor thought the baby was stillborn; while the physician attended to Dolly, one of the baby's grandmothers put the child under the cold-water faucet and shocked him to life.

The infant was baptized as Frank Sinestro; a few years later, the family name was changed to Sinatra. Still later, Sinatra changed his given names to Francis Albert.

Frank Sinatra as a boy. Sinatra was born in 1915 in Hoboken, New Jersey.

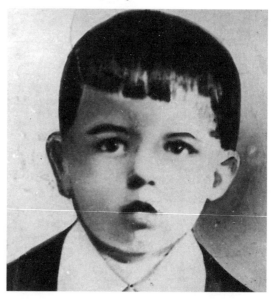

Times were tough for the Sinatras, and both adults did what they could for money. The burly Marty first tried his luck at prizefighting under the name Marty O'Brien. (It was commonly believed that Irish fighters had a better chance at success than Italians in Irish-dominated Hoboken.) After thirty fights, however, Marty broke his wrists and had to quit. He lost a second job on the docks because of his chronic asthma, but in 1927 found work as a fireman.

Marty was quiet, gentle, and passive. He was also nearly illiterate, unable to read or to write much more than his name. By all accounts, however, Marty Sinatra was a sweet and considerate man, and his son idolized him. Years later the singer remarked, "Oh, but he was a lovely, lovely man. I adored him. In some ways, the greatest man I ever knew in my life."[6]

Hoboken fire captain Marty Sinatra playfully puts his hat on his son Frank's head.

A RAP AND A HUG

In contrast to her husband, Dolly Sinatra was a tireless, outgoing ball of energy. She held a variety of jobs, including dipping chocolates and running a bar called Marty O'Brien's. She was also a midwife and an occasional abortionist. This last occupation was not only illegal but scandalous in the Sinatra's largely Catholic community, and as Frank grew older it became a source of great shame for him.

But the job at which Dolly really excelled was as a political string-puller for the local Democratic Party. She was a ward-heeler— that is, a "fixer" who vigorously encouraged newly arrived immigrants in her neighborhood to vote for certain candidates. In exchange for these votes, Dolly and her Democratic partners could offer a variety of practical help: money for groceries and fuel, perhaps, or aid in keeping a wayward child out of trouble.

Marty's job as a fireman and his eventual rise to captain despite the fact that he never took a written exam were directly due to Dolly's political clout. She eventually rose in power until she led the Third Ward of Hoboken's Ninth District; she was probably the first Italian American to hold such a position in a town dominated by politicians of Irish and German descent, and she was almost certainly the first woman.

GETTING STARTED

Marian Bush Schrieber, a friend of Sinatra's in his teenage years, recalls in this passage Sinatra's first experiences in singing publicly in the early 1930s. The quote is from Will Friedwald's Sinatra: The Song Is You: A Singer's Art.

"[Frank] didn't have a job at the time, but he loved hanging around musicians, so I suggested that he get an orchestra together for our Wednesday night dances. In exchange for hiring the musicians, he'd get to sing a few numbers with the band. I'd take the money at the door, and when we got enough, we all went to the Village Inn in New York so that Frank could sing with the orchestra there. We'd go in to ask the manager beforehand to let Frankie sing. We said that was the only way we would come in (being under age), and so he usually said yes. Frank did such a good job for our school dances on Wednesday that he wanted to take the orchestra to Our Lady of Grace for their Friday night dances, but the Irish Catholics wouldn't let him in . . . because of the scandals involving his mother, Natalie (Dolly). They would have nothing to do with him."

Dolly got things done, but at a price; she was a selfish tyrant and a bully obsessed with power and control. She spoke a rough form of street English and every dialect of Italian known in her neighborhood, and in all of them her foul mouth was legendary. All of these were traits that would appear in the adult Frank Sinatra, as biographer Donald Clarke points out: "Dolly [was] the only benchmark he had all his life, her attitudes the only ones he had ever learned, the only ones he measured himself against."[7]

She was just as controlling within her family as in the neighborhood in general. Marty went along with whatever she said, and the relatives who sometimes came from Italy to live with the family were just as submissive. Late in Sinatra's life, the singer freely admitted that his mother had always terrified him; he evoked the love-hate relationship he had with her all his life by recalling the short billy club she kept behind the bar at Marty O'Brien's saloon: "When I would get out of hand, she would give me a rap with that little club; then she'd hug me to her breast."[8]

LONELY KID

Frank, an only child, was a loner from an early age. Marty was away all day, and so passive when home that he was barely noticed. Dolly was always away herself, taking care of some business or other.

When he was not in school, Frank spent hours by himself, wandering in the streets or looked after at home by his grandmothers. In his solitude, he yearned for a bigger family. "I used to wish I had an older brother that could help me when I needed him," Sinatra once said. "I wished I had a younger sister I could protect. But I didn't. It was Dolly, Marty, and me."[9]

Nonetheless, Frank had plenty of friends, at least partly because the Sinatras were better off financially than many of their neighbors. The Great Depression had come in 1929, and very few families had spare cash.

One way in which Dolly tried to compensate for her frequent absences was by pampering her child; Frank always had plenty of pocket money, and he liked to buy other kids treats like ice-cream cones or movie tickets. He had his own charge account at a local department store, his own phonograph player, and so many pairs of trousers that neighbor kids nicknamed him "Slacksie O'Brien."

By 1932 the family had saved enough to move to their own house on 841 Garden Street, and it was, by the standards of the day, a comfortable place; it boasted central heating, indoor plumbing, and

Sinatra with his mother, Dolly. Dolly Sinatra held considerable political clout in Hoboken, where she was known as a tough-talking, domineering figure.

enough rooms that the Sinatras could take in boarders. There was even a telephone. In the depths of the Depression, this was prosperity indeed.

The household also included an example of a new form of technology, the wireless radio, that was dramatically affecting American life and culture. After its introduction in the early 1920s, radio became a vital source of information, education, and entertainment for virtually everyone, from wealthy city dwellers to isolated rural families and poor immigrants. The Sinatra family was no exception, and the radio was a crucial part of young Frank's early musical education. "The radio was like a religion," Sinatra remembers of those days. "They were even shaped like cathedrals."[10]

Frank was never an enthusiastic student. He graduated from junior high in 1931 but finished only forty-seven days of high school before dropping out. He was fifteen. Dolly found Frank a job working on a delivery truck for the *Jersey Observer* newspaper, where the boy's godfather and namesake, Frank Garrick, was the circulation manager.

Sinatra inherited many traits from his mother, including bravado and the capacity to carry a grudge. When the teenager heard that the *Observer*'s sportswriter had died, he sat down at the late reporter's desk and told other reporters that he was the new sportswriter. The bluff lasted only until his godfather heard about it. Garrick fired Sinatra from his delivery job, and both mother and son stopped speaking to Garrick—a silence that lasted for over fifty years. "My son is like me," Dolly once remarked. "You cross him, he never forgets."[11]

EARLY LESSONS

All his life, Sinatra was an outspoken advocate of racial and ethnic equality. In this excerpt from Pete Hamill's Why Sinatra Matters, *Hamill and his subject reflect on Sinatra's early lessons in injustice.*

"Partly, of course, this isolation was because he was a pampered only child. However, in part it was also because he was part of an ethnic minority that was looked down on by many. Sinatra's encounters with prejudice as a child would go far in fostering his later liberal tendencies as well as his stubborn pride and violent temper. 'Of course, it meant something to me to be the son of immigrants,' he later remarked. 'How could it not? . . . I grew up for a few years thinking I was just another American kid. Then I discovered at—what? five? six?—I discovered that some people thought I was a dago. A wop. A guinea.'"

THE CROSBY INFLUENCE

The idea of becoming a singer first occurred to Sinatra at about age eleven. Marty O'Brien's saloon had a player piano, and occasionally a patron would pick the boy up and put him on the piano. Later in his life, Sinatra reflected, "I'd sing along with the music on the roll. One day, I got a nickel. I said, 'This is the racket.'"[12]

As Sinatra grew he developed a pleasant voice, but he did not become serious about singing until sometime in the early 1930s. Accounts vary as to the details, but the turning point came in 1930 or 1931, in a town in New Jersey or in New York City. One thing is for certain: a performance by Bing Crosby set Sinatra on the path to a singing career. He later recalled, "You can't imagine how big Crosby was. He was the biggest thing in the country. On records. On the radio. In the movies. Everybody wanted to be Bing Crosby, including me."[13]

Sinatra had seen Crosby movies for years and was certainly familiar with the older man's inimitable way of crooning a tune. But seeing Crosby in person was a turning point; after the show, Sinatra decided that he could do that, too. From then on, a career in singing became Frank's unshakable goal. This was more than just a pipe dream; it was a potential means to leave Hoboken. In those days, young men in Sinatra's neighborhood were almost inevitably destined to a lifetime of working in a factory or some similar low-level job. A singing career, Sinatra could see, was one way to escape.

Marty disapproved of the notion and urged his son to attend Hoboken's Stevens Institute of Technology with an eye toward becoming an engineer. But the real opposition came from Dolly; she hated the idea of Frank singing for a living so much that she reportedly tore down a picture of Crosby from Frank's bedroom wall, threw a shoe at it, and called Crosby several choice names.

Dolly kept at Frank mercilessly to give up his idea. During the standoff between mother and son over his choice of career, Frank even moved out temporarily. Many years later, the singer bitterly commented, "There's always someone to spit on your dreams."[14]

THE HOBOKEN FOUR

Frank could be as bullheaded as his mother, however. He could not afford formal lessons, but he began studying other singers to see how they achieved certain effects. Recognizing that physical fitness was important to maintain singing stamina, the small but wiry Sinatra also began swimming at a local pool and running on the track at a nearby school.

Dolly had a change of heart when it became clear that her son truly had his heart set on singing. She then put all her formidable energy into helping him and used her connections to arrange performances. As a result, Sinatra got chances to sing at roadhouse taverns, political fund-raisers, the odd radio broadcast, and any other place that would take him. He was so eager for opportunities to perform that he often sang for nothing more than streetcar fare.

"SOMEDAY . . ."

Nancy Barbato, later Sinatra's first wife, remembers the night she and Frank heard a show by his hero, Bing Crosby (in a passage from her daughter Nancy's book Frank Sinatra: An American Legend*).*

"It was a very exciting evening for both of us, but for Frank it was the biggest moment of his life. Bing had always been his hero, and he had listened to all his records, but watching him perform in person seemed to make it all come alive for him. I mean, he loved to sing; he'd sing at parties, he sang for me all the time, and he used to take me along on some of his appearances around town. But I don't think he really believed it, I don't think he believed it would ever really happen for him, until that night. 'Someday,' he told me, 'that's gonna be me up there.'"

Bing Crosby, the performer who inspired Sinatra to seriously pursue a singing career.

Dolly also bought her son a portable public address system, so that he could be heard above bands and in noisy nightclubs. Since Sinatra would later become an unparalleled master of using the microphone to achieve dramatic effects, this marked a genuine turning point. "This was the equivalent of buying a trumpet for Miles Davis," notes journalist Pete Hamill. "Frank Sinatra had his instrument at last."[15]

At the age of nineteen, Frank joined an established singing group. The Three Flashes—James "Skelly" Petrozelli, Pat Principe, and Fred Tamburro—were far more experienced than the skinny young Sinatra. According to legend, Frank was chosen because he had a car; the others were skeptical of the newcomer's talent but needed the kid to drive them to gigs.

Their break came in September 1935, when the group—now known as the Hoboken Four—appeared on *Major Bowes' Original Amateur Hour*, a top-rated radio show that popularized the catchphrase "the wheel of fortune spins, and where she stops, nobody knows." Major Bowes, the host of the show, specialized in presenting new, untested talent. The winning act in each broadcast, as chosen by the studio audience, was awarded a promotional tour organized by Major Bowes.

"How About It?"

The broadcast introducing the Hoboken Four took place at the Capitol Theater in New York City. Sinatra, exuding confidence, jauntily introduced the group by saying, "I'm Frank, Major. We're looking for jobs. How about it?"[16]

He got his wish: The Hoboken Four won the contest that night with their performance of "Shine," a song made popular by the Mills Brothers. As a result, the group went on a brief tour with other *Amateur Hour* winners, traveling as far as California. The performers sang not just in regional theaters but also in grocery stores; the radio program's sponsor (also the sponsor of the tour) was a coffee company.

Sinatra (far right) got his big break when he performed on the Major Bowes' Original Amateur Hour *radio show in 1935 as part of the Hoboken Four.*

By this time, Sinatra had so improved as a vocalist that he had become the Hoboken Four's lead singer. He was already especially popular with young women in their audiences, too, which may have hastened a parting of the ways; he had never gotten along well with the others in the group, and they may have resented his burgeoning popularity.

Whatever the reason, by the end of 1935 Sinatra was no longer a member of the Hoboken Four. After the split, he returned to singing wherever possible but did not get a regular singing job until 1938, when Sinatra was hired as a singing waiter at the Rustic Cabin, a New Jersey roadhouse just across the George Washington Bridge from Manhattan. The gig paid $15 a week and involved a little bit of everything; he later recalled: "I never stopped. I showed people to tables, I sang with the band, I sang in between sets."[17]

Until this point, Sinatra was entirely self-taught. Now, however, he began taking lessons from a former opera singer, John Quinlan, to improve his style, range,

Frank Sinatra (center) and his first wife Nancy Barbato Sinatra, whom he married in February 1939.

and phrasing. Quinlan also gave Sinatra lessons in diction; the Jersey boy was acutely aware of how rough his speaking voice sounded between songs.

The Rustic Cabin was a good location for an aspiring singer because radio station WNEW used it to broadcast a popular dance music show live on Saturday nights. This was valuable exposure, and as a result Sinatra began getting work elsewhere as well. He also began singing several times a week on other WNEW music shows.

Love and Marriage

In 1938 Sinatra's popularity with women resulted in his first brush with the law, when he was arrested on a morals charge. Over sixty years later, details are hazy, but it seems that a woman he was seeing became pregnant; he dumped her, and she got revenge by convincing the police to arrest him. Sinatra was never prosecuted, however, perhaps because of his mother's influence in local politics. In any event, following the incident Dolly could see the handwriting on the wall, and she decided her son could stay out of trouble by becoming a married man.

Off and on since 1935, Sinatra had been dating Nancy Barbato, a striking, dark-haired young woman who lived across the street from one of his aunts in Long Branch, New Jersey. Now, urged on by Dolly, things became more serious between them, and in February 1939 Sinatra and Nancy Barbato were wed.

The day before the wedding, Sinatra made his first record: "Our Love," backed by a local band, the Frank Manne Orchestra. It was never released commercially and was probably meant as a demo record. But it can also be seen as a wedding present for his new bride.

The couple settled into a three-room apartment in Jersey City. Between Frank's income and Nancy's salary as a secretary, they earned about $200 a month—not bad in a nation still suffering from the Depression.

After Sinatra moved in with his new wife, he would never again live in Hoboken. In fact, he only returned there twice in his life. He accepted the key to the city in 1947, after his initial burst of stardom. But he would not come back until 1985, when he received an honorary doctorate from the city's Stevens Institute. Hoboken was a nowhere town as far as Sinatra was concerned, and he was happy to be out of it. He had more ambitious plans in mind.

2 On the Road with Harry and Tommy

You could almost feel the excitement coming up out of the crowds when that kid stood up to sing.

—bandleader Tommy Dorsey

In the decades before World War II, singers outside the classical field were generally not solo acts; their only way to fame was as a "boy singer" or "girl singer" in a band. Few vocalists were popular enough to stand alone; Bing Crosby was a rare exception. Typically, audiences came to dance to a band, not to listen to a singer; a band's vocalist would sing only a few songs in an evening, as a special feature rather than an evening's entire entertainment.

Sinatra's first big break came through this route of band singing. In 1939 Harry James, a lanky Texan who had been a star trumpet soloist in Benny Goodman's popular swing band, left Goodman to put together his own orchestra—and he needed singers.

James's wife, singer Louise Tobin, heard Sinatra on the radio and thought he'd work well in her husband's new band. So James went to the Rustic Cabin in June 1939 to check Sinatra out. He liked what he heard and offered the singer $75 a week. The ambitious Sinatra eagerly ac-

cepted; many years later he recalled about meeting James, "When he left Benny Goodman and came over to see me, I almost broke his arm so he wouldn't get away, 'cause I was dying to get out of that place!"[18]

ALMOST FRANKIE SATIN

At first, James wanted to give his singer a new name, one that was blander and less obviously ethnic. Sinatra refused, however, and told James that if he wanted the voice he had to take the name too: "He wanted me to call myself Frankie *Satin*! . . . If I'd've done that, I'd be working cruise ships today."[19]

The James band was versatile, able to play both the current dance styles, sweet and hot, equally well. James was an astute judge of talent, moreover, and picked a group of crack musicians adept at soloing as well as ensemble playing.

Singing with the James band thus provided valuable on-the-job training for the relatively inexperienced Sinatra. He had a chance every night to study how the musicians in the band used their instruments to convey emotion and rhythmic swing. Louise Tobin, James's wife, once commented: "In six months with Harry, Frank learned more about music than he'd known in his life up to that point."[20]

Sinatra himself loved his time with James and found the experience inspiring in general. He later remembered, "With Harry, for the first time in my life I was with people who thought the sky was the limit. They thought they could go to the top, and that's what they aimed for. They didn't all make it, but what the hell. They knew the only direction was up."[21]

Sinatra and James got along very well and forged a friendship that lasted until James's death in 1983. They were almost the same age, and they were both extremely self-confident and ambitious. Both were also notably skinny; a wag once remarked that together they looked like a pair of scissors.

Between July and November 1939, Sinatra recorded ten tunes with the Harry James Orchestra, his first professional recordings. He also got one of his first notices in print; a writer for the music magazine *Metronome* commented in a review on Sinatra's "very pleasing vocals" and "easy phrasing."[22]

In addition to recording, Sinatra also went on the road with James. Taking

Trumpet player Harry James (pictured) recruited Sinatra to sing with the Harry James Orchestra in 1939.

Nancy with him, he traveled to the West Coast and back with the band, but business was poor. The band was hot and Sinatra loved traveling with the musicians, but the Harry James Orchestra was failing to set the musical world on fire.

"THE OLD MAN"

While the James band was in Chicago to perform for the annual musicians' union Christmas benefit, late in 1939, Sinatra received his second big break. Also in Chicago for the performance was Tommy Dorsey, one of the nation's top bandleaders.

Dorsey's popular male vocalist, Jack Leonard, had just quit, and the band needed a replacement fast. The bandleader was aware of Sinatra's talent, and he offered the singer $125 a week. It was an offer the singer couldn't turn down; Nancy was pregnant, he needed to think hard about his finances, and Harry James couldn't afford to pay even Sinatra's $75 a week salary. Sinatra debuted with the Dorsey band early in 1940.

Sinatra hated to leave James's band, however. Many times in the years since, the singer remarked that he'd "rather have opened a vein" than leave that group. The parting was amicable, although Sinatra later revealed his great sadness at the split in a comment that reveals something of the singer's deep need to belong:

> The bus pulled out with the rest of the boys at about half-past midnight. I'd said good-bye to them all, and it was

snowing, I remember. There was nobody around and I stood alone with my suitcase in the snow and watched the taillights disappear. Then the tears started and I tried to run after the bus.[23]

Tommy Dorsey was not only a bandleader but also a gifted trombonist and a savvy businessman who was succeeding well in a cutthroat business. Like James, Dorsey also had a knack for spotting talent: Around the time Sinatra joined the band, Dorsey also hired several other gifted performers, including

Sinatra (right) left James's band to join forces with Tommy Dorsey (left).

Dorsey (left) with Sinatra (center) and the Pied Pipers.

arranger Sy Oliver, trumpeter Bunny Berigan, singer Connie Haines, drummer Buddy Rich, and the Pied Pipers, a vocal quartet whose lead singer was the superb Jo Stafford.

A decade older than Sinatra and many of his musicians, Dorsey was known to the band as "the Old Man." He was a tough, exacting boss who demanded much from his musicians and brooked no nonsense from them. Sinatra often remarked in the years since that Dorsey was almost a father to him, and when Sinatra's first child, Nancy, was born later in 1940 he asked Dorsey to be her godfather.

Singer Jo Stafford was a veteran pro by the time she joined Dorsey and her standards were high, but she was immediately struck by the less experienced Sinatra's gifts. In an era when virtually every "boy singer" tried to sound like Bing Crosby, here was somebody who was different. She later recalled about their initial encounter:

> Frank joined the band while we were playing a theater in Milwaukee. The Pipers were . . . well, we thought we were pretty good. We were a little clique unto ourselves. Frank was very thin in those days, almost fragile looking. When he stepped up to the microphone, we all smirked and looked at each other, waiting to see what he could do. The first song he did was "Stardust."

> I know it sounds like something out of a B movie, but it's true: before he'd sung four bars, we *knew*. We knew he was going to be a great star.[24]

PUTTING ON A SHOW

Sinatra learned many things from his time with the Tommy Dorsey Orchestra. Here (quoted in Pete Hamill's Why Sinatra Matters*) he reflects on Dorsey's ability to orchestrate an exciting and fulfilling evening's worth of music.*

"He put together a show like it was one long piece of music, or like an album—this was before the LP, and you couldn't do records that way—with different moods and movements leading to a crescendo. He knew how to shift a mood so it didn't all sound the same and bore the ass off the audience. It was dance music, first and foremost. But it was more than that. I always kept that in mind later, for my own shows and albums. Tommy didn't spell it out to us, but he didn't have to. It became part of you, just from doing it. Seven shows a day, sometimes, if you worked a theater. Three shows a night, if the gig was a dance somewhere. It became part of you."

"WITHOUT BREAD AND WATER, MAN!"

According to Joe Bushkin, then the pianist for Dorsey, Frank Sinatra's real trial by fire with his formidable new backing group came during his New York nightclub debut, at the grand reopening of the fashionable Astor Roof, in May 1940. A star-studded audience that included Benny Goodman and pianist/composer/actor Oscar Levant watched Sinatra stop the show with his version of the Cole Porter standard "Begin the Beguine."

The audience called loudly for more. Dorsey was happy to ride the wave of their approval, but he had no other Sinatra features in his band book. He instructed the band to play a popular song of the day, "Polka Dots and Moonbeams," and the crowd went wild. Dorsey then told Sinatra to sing whatever he wanted to with only Bushkin backing him.

The pianist and Sinatra went into a piano-voice duet. Sinatra instructed Bushkin to play a few tunes, including Jerome Kern's "All the Things You Are," but the twenty-three-year-old pianist was struggling. Bushkin was unfamiliar with the new singer's possibilities, and as he played he was desperately trying to figure out Sinatra's range so that he could back him properly.

Then the singer turned around and said, "Smoke Gets in Your Eyes," naming another famous tune by Kern. It is a notoriously difficult song, one whose harmonic changes have tripped up many a singer—and many a pianist as well.

Bushkin remembered his own failure but Sinatra's self-confident forging ahead at this crucial moment:

Unless you really know what you're doing, that chord change will just lose you. I'm right out there without bread and water, man! Next thing I know, Frank was out there singing it all by himself, *a cappella*. I was so embarrassed. . . . [A]ll the guys were looking at me, so I just turned around and walked away from the piano! And that was the last song we did. I thought Tommy was going to kill me, but [instead] he thought it was so funny. And *that* is the night Frank Sinatra happened.[25]

INFLUENCES

Sinatra was unlike run-of-the-mill singers, in large part, because he was listening carefully to a wide range of musicians and musical styles. For example, he learned a great deal by listening to violin virtuoso Jascha Heifetz, who ruled the concert stage for many years. He was also a serious student of the exquisite sense of timing and phrasing perfected by the sublime jazz singers Billie Holiday and Mabel Mercer.

But his biggest influence was the trombone playing of Tommy Dorsey himself. Sitting on the bandstand nightly, Sinatra was struck by Dorsey's ability to play long phrases without apparently taking a breath. The singer realized that Dorsey had perfected a style of breathing in which he would take "sips" of air from one side of his mouth. (This is not so-called circular breathing, a technique some horn players use to inhale through the nose while exhaling through the

mouth.) Dorsey constantly emphasized the importance of such stamina to his sidemen; the band's lead alto saxophonist, Arthur "Skeets" Herfurt, once recalled, "Tommy sometimes used to make the whole orchestra (not just the trombones) play from the top of a page down to the bottom without taking a breath."[26]

Sinatra quickly realized that an ability to sing long, flowing phrases would set him apart from most singers, who did not have such stamina and tended to sing in much shorter phrases. He stepped up his regimen of running and swimming lengths underwater to improve his wind capacity.

Dorsey (right) motivated Sinatra (left) to improve his singing stamina.

Life on the road with Dorsey taught him other things as well. Traveling the country in the band bus and appearing onstage at odd hours throughout the day and night taught Sinatra the usefulness of taking short naps whenever possible. This ability served the singer well in later years, when chronic insomnia and restlessness often kept him up all night. (Also during his time with Dorsey, Sinatra was introduced to marijuana; he did not like it, however, and disdained it for the rest of his life.)

Mostly, however, life with the Dorsey band taught Sinatra a sense of professionalism. The singer remembered of those times,

> When it comes to professional experience, there's nothing to beat those one-nighter tours, when you rotate between five places around the clock—the bus, your hotel room, the greasy-spoon restaurant, the dressing room (if any), and the bandstand. Then back on the bus to the next night's gig, maybe four hundred miles away or more.[27]

"A Skinny Kid with Big Ears"

Gradually, Sinatra took a more and more prominent role in the Dorsey organization, eclipsing even the other talented performers in the bandleader's stable. By May 1940, when the band was performing at New York City's Astor Hotel, Sinatra was regularly stopping the show as audiences called out for encores—a very unusual occurrence for a mere "boy singer." Clearly, something unusual was also happening to the women in the audience when Sinatra took the stage. Dorsey once remarked, "Remember, he was no matinee idol. He was a skinny kid with big ears. And yet what he did to women was something awful."[28]

Touring the country with the band, Sinatra quickly became a star. By May 1941 the trade magazine *Billboard* had named him the nation's top male singer, and by the end of the year he had pushed even the mighty Bing Crosby out of the top slot in *Down Beat* magazine's readers' poll.

"You Know, Normal."

Life on the road with Harry James and Tommy Dorsey was hardly a regular existence. In a passage from Hamill's Why Sinatra Matters, *Sinatra remembers the strangeness of his life.*

"I'd be in the bus, and the guys'd be sleeping or drinking or talking. And I'd look out the window and see these houses with the lights on and wonder how they all lived. The houses looked warm. Safe. You know, *normal*. I was still a kid, but I knew that it was too late for me to have that kind of life."

As a rising young star on tour with Dorsey's band, Sinatra wowed audiences nationwide.

In January 1942, with members of Dorsey's band, Sinatra made his first four recordings under his own name; the material included Jerome Kern's "The Song Is You" and Cole Porter's "Night and Day," two standards that would remain in Sinatra's repertoire for the rest of his career. They were issued on the Bluebird label, the budget-priced division of Dorsey's label, Victor Records. All were arranged by Axel Stordahl, who had joined Dorsey's payroll a few years before Sinatra and who would later become a vital part of the singer's career.

MOVING ON

Sinatra knew, far in advance of the fact, that he would leave Dorsey eventually. He was eager to move on, and he had the bold idea that he could strike out on his own as a solo act.

The bandleader hated to have people quit; it upset his sense of being in control. So in September 1941 Sinatra gave Dorsey a year's notice of his intention to leave, instead of the usual two weeks. Typically, Dorsey simply ignored the warning and seemed genuinely shocked when Sinatra did leave the band in August 1942.

The band was busy, meanwhile: a grueling schedule of live appearances, frequent guest spots or headlining roles on radio shows, even a brief appearance in a mostly forgettable Hollywood movie called *Ship Ahoy*.

But the Dorsey-Sinatra team's most lasting success was in recording. They recorded about ninety songs together between February 1940 and July 1942; many were big hits, and most still sound fresh today. While most of the recordings were performed with the full orchestra, others were done with a smaller group; one of the latter, "I'll Never Smile Again," stayed at the number one spot on the music charts for twelve weeks.

Anxious to escape his contract, Sinatra signed a termination arrangement he would soon regret. He agreed to pay Dorsey a third of his gross earnings for the next ten years—an outrageously good deal for Dorsey. In the summer of 1943, after Sinatra's solo career really took off, the singer forced Dorsey to renegotiate. There have long been rumors of underworld involvement here; even in the early days, Sinatra's reputation for associating with mobsters was well established. However, there has never been any proof of coercion in the negotiations, and it was probably simply a matter of the lawyers for both parties working out a more realistic agreement.

Under the new agreement, Dorsey got $60,000 from Sinatra plus a small percentage for the next five years. The ill feeling created between singer and bandleader took a long time to dissipate. "He's one of the most fascinating men in the world," Dorsey once said bitterly, "but don't stick your hand in the cage."[29]

Not until a decade later, in 1956, when Dorsey was very ill, did the two appear onstage again briefly; but then, after Dorsey's death, Sinatra declined to perform on a television tribute to the bandleader. Nonetheless, late in his career Sinatra often reminisced to friends at length about "the Old Man" and what he had meant to the singer.

When Sinatra left Dorsey in the summer of '42, the news hardly made a ripple in the overall music industry. The two were popular musicians, but the split was not a shocking event; singers changed bands all the time. Dorsey replaced Sinatra with another talented singer, Dick Haymes, and, for a while, life went on.

But Sinatra was making good on his plans for a solo career, typically full of confidence. Then it began to take off as nobody had expected.

Chapter

3 Swoonatra!

Just as Benny Goodman's 1935–36 band made the public orchestra-conscious, so did Frank's rise to fame usher in a new era of popular music, a vocalist's era.

—singer Mel Tormé

Going solo was risky business for a band singer; others, including former Dorseyite Jack Leonard, had tried it with little success. But Sinatra had no doubts.

In planning the details of his career, Sinatra left little to chance. Along with his singing lessons, he added ballet lessons to refine his onstage hand gestures and elocution lessons to improve his speech. He also became keenly interested in the financial side of his career, putting into practice what he had learned from Dorsey about business savvy and self-promotion.

Interested in resuming his involvement with movies, Sinatra moved to Los Angeles. This proved premature, however; the only role he secured in Hollywood was in the now-forgotten *Reveille with Beverly*. With his base on the West Coast, Sinatra's singing career likewise stalled, and he had to return to the East Coast more or less full-time to find engagements. It was here that the singer landed the gig that made him a household word.

THE FIRST PARAMOUNT SHOWS

Sinatra's rise to fame began in earnest when an employee of his booking agency, General Amusement Corporation, talked the manager of a major venue, New York's Paramount Theater, into catching Sinatra's act at a small theater in New Jersey. The Paramount owner was impressed and booked the singer as an "extra added attraction" for a 1942 New Year's Eve show with Benny Goodman's swing band headlining.

The celebration at the Paramount quickly turned to pandemonium. Women audience members had been swooning over Sinatra for some time; but the crowd went wild that New Year's Eve. This frenzied reaction was mostly, but not entirely, spontaneous. George Evans, Sinatra's canny new public relations man, admitted years later that he had hired a dozen young women to scream and swoon—but hundreds more obligingly shrieked *without* being paid.

Women pack the Paramount Theater in New York during Sinatra's October 1944 performance. The hysterical fans created such pandemonium that police and reserves had to be called in.

When Sinatra took the stage, the applause drowned out the orchestra, and girls immediately began screaming and rushing the stage. Yank Lawson, then a trumpeter in Goodman's band, recalled that the older bandleader was shocked, but that he himself and the other younger band members loved it: "The applause was so great, and all those kids were dancing in the aisles. We thought it was great!"[30]

Sinatra was hardly the first entertainer to create hysterical reactions among fans—Bing Crosby and the silent-screen idol Rudolph Valentino Jr. are two examples just from the twentieth century. Nor was he the last. Still, no one had seen adulation of this intensity before.

Immediately following the first Paramount show, the singer was booked for an extended engagement at the theater, performing six shows a day (a common practice in those days); for every show, the lines snaked around the block. Within a month, the singer's weekly salary went from $750 to $25,000. He was suddenly the hottest act in the nation.

When Sinatra returned to the Paramount in October 1944 for another three-week stand, the lines formed before dawn. Some thirty thousand fans milled outside the theater, and those with tickets for the later shows became frenzied when the previous show's patrons wouldn't leave. Many fans insisted on sitting through all five shows. At one point, a near-riot erupted; windows were broken and traffic was stopped. Two hundred policemen and four hundred reserves were called in to restore order.

WHAT THEY WANTED TO SEE

Francis Davis—in his Atlantic *magazine piece "Missing from Much of the Recent Commentary on Frank Sinatra, Oddly, Was One Pertinent Topic: What He Meant for Music"—has this to say about Sinatra's uncanny ability to appeal to young women.*

"His initial appeal to teenage girls of the 1940s was comparable to that of Leonardo DiCaprio to pre-teen girls in our quicker, more jaded day. The young Sinatra came across as a boy who might try to sweet-talk a girl into going all the way but wasn't going to be insistent—unlike the boys his fans knew in real life, most of whom were desperate not to march off to war still virgins. Indulgent parents perceived Sinatra as safe, and so did many of their daughters. Often what young girls want in a boy is another girl, and the girls who swooned over Sinatra pressed him to their hearts as a young man who was as sensitive and, on some level, as self-conscious as they were."

Police officers hold back a crowd of young women eager to get near the beloved singer. Sinatra was one of the first celebrities to inspire such heights of adoration from female fans.

The Voice

George Evans, the public relations man, and the press together invented dozens of words like "Swoonatra" and "Sinatrauma" to describe what was going on. They made up nicknames for the singer like "the Sultan of Swoon." For many fans, however, the simplest nickname was the most telling: to them, Sinatra was simply "the Voice."

The appeal mystified many observers. Who was this skinny, frail-looking kid with the floppy bow tie? People joked that Sinatra was so thin that if he stood side-

Sinatra's boyish good looks and charm earned him nicknames like "the Sultan of Swoon."

ways, he disappeared behind the mike stand. What made him so special? To his fans, it seemed crystal clear.

It was, of course, first and foremost the voice. In an era before television made visual images all important, the quality of a singer's voice was crucial. The words of a song heard on the radio or a record evoked powerful, private images from the listener's imagination. Sinatra's elegant long phrasing, subtle sense of rhythm, and perfect diction made every word clear as a bell, and he sang with such conviction that his fans had no trouble believing in him.

Radio broadcasts and records were not everything, however. Live performance was still an important part of a singer's life. As a solo artist, he now had to fill the entire star spot—forty minutes to an hour per show—all by himself; no more was he just a "featured singer" for three or four songs. Unlike most singers who came of age in the big band era, Sinatra had the necessary charisma to pull this off.

For one thing, Sinatra recognized the importance of visual impact, and he turned himself into a master dramatist. Each song became a mini-drama, a complete story. Since the songs he sang were generally ones with lyrics that touched him personally, he was able to convincingly convey their emotional power.

Sinatra may have been a high school dropout, but he had an almost literary insight into lyrics. In biographer John Lahr's opinion, no one told better stories:

> With other singers . . . you admired the technique; with Sinatra you admired the rendition. He represented

the song like a landscape he'd restored, painting himself into the picture so masterfully that it was impossible to imagine himself without it.[31]

Sinatra also recognized the importance of using the microphone as if it were an instrument, one that could be played as carefully and subtly as a violin, sax, or piano. Careful use of the mike gave Sinatra the ability to create an intimate feeling even in a large theater; he could sound as if he were singing softly in the ear of every person there. The great *New Yorker* writer E. B. White once noted, "To Sinatra, a microphone is as real as a girl waiting to be kissed."[32]

Sinatra's microphone use fostered a sense of personal connection with his audience.

"A GREAT LONELINESS"

Another aspect of Sinatra's appeal lay in the complex image he projected as a young man. In the early 1940s and throughout the years of World War II, Sinatra's image was a mixture of vulnerability and self-confidence; although he was in control of every aspect of his performance, he also seemed frail and exposed. He seemed to need someone to care for him.

This persona appealed, clearly, mostly to young female fans, sometimes nicknamed bobby-soxers. These loyal fans formed clubs with names like the Slaves of Sinatra, the Sighing Society of Sinatra Swooners, the Flatbush Girls Who Would Lay Down Their Lives for Frank Sinatra. They collected "Frankie-boy's" records and memo-rabilia obsessively. They held "swooning parties" in which they practiced fainting over their idol. They even fought over footprints the singer made in the snow, which they took home and kept frozen.

But Sinatra appealed to males as well. The punctured eardrum suffered at birth kept him from enlisting in the military, but he was able to appear on USO tours entertaining American troops. He feared these audiences would be hostile, resenting his lack of a uniform. But he won them over by casting himself as the underdog; he made fun of his skinny frame between songs, emphasized his blue-collar origins, and created a persona that the grizzled soldiers could identify with.

And, of course, the voice and the songs appealed to men as well. One of his signature tunes, "Nancy (With the Laughin' Face)," had been written by friends of the singer as a tribute to his young daughter; but the sentimental song proved to be a huge hit with lonely servicemen during the war. To them, it spoke yearningly of faraway wives, girlfriends, or daughters.

To the singer himself, the secret of his appeal was simple:

> Psychologists have tried to go into the reasons why. With all sorts of theories. I could have told them why. Perfectly simple: It was the war years, and there was a great loneliness. I was the boy in every corner drugstore, the boy who'd gone off to war.[33]

THE LUCKY STRIKE

Sinatra did not let up on the momentum created by his initial burst of fame. His work pattern throughout the 1940s involved at least two live radio shows per week, performances at theaters in the daytime and nightclubs at night, the occasional benefit, regular recording, and at least one film per year.

The radio shows included *Broadway Bandbox* and his own fifteen-minute program, *Songs by Sinatra*. In 1943 the singer joined the cast of one of the nation's most popular shows, *Your Hit Parade*, which unveiled a new set of top tunes every week. While appearing on it, Sinatra was invited to the White House to meet his political idol, Franklin D. Roosevelt. After the introductions, FDR (who was in a wheelchair) beckoned the young singer

to lean down to him. "Psst, Frank," the president whispered. "I promise not to tell anyone. What's number one this Saturday?"[34]

One factor in Sinatra's success as a solo artist was simply lucky timing. The American Federation of Musicians, the musicians' union, went on strike against record companies in 1942. This labor action was a boon to vocalists everywhere, since only instrumentalists could be union members.

Thus singers were exempt from the strike, during which musicians were forbidden to make records. Musicians and radio station owners hated the strike, a last-ditch attempt to ban records from radio; despite pleas from these camps, however, it dragged on for two years.

In the end, only vocalists benefited; they could simply begin making records a cappella, without instrumental accompaniment. Music fans gradually began paying attention to individual singers, not just to bandleaders or songs as they had in years past. The change helped usher in an era of popular music in which the vocalist was the prime force. Needless to say, popular music's number one vocalist benefited more than anyone.

COLLABORATORS

During the strike, Sinatra recorded several songs backed only by a vocal chorus for his new label, Columbia. In addition, the songs he had recorded with Harry James were reissued to cash in on the singer's fame. When the strike ended late in 1944, Sinatra made his first full-blown recordings in two years. The music from this session—which included "Saturday Night (Is the Loneliest Night of the Week)" and "I Fall in Love Too Easily," two songs that remained in Sinatra's repertoire all his life—marks his partnerships with two significant collaborators.

Manie Sachs was the Columbia A&R (artist and repertoire) man assigned to Sinatra. A&R personnel matched artists with material, filling roles often taken today by producers. Sachs and Sinatra worked well together, forming a friendship that lasted until Sachs's death in 1958.

Arranger Axel Stordahl had left Dorsey to join Sinatra's solo venture, with a pay increase from $130 to $650 a week. For the Columbia recordings, Stordahl created string-laden, understated foils for Sinatra's carefully nuanced vocals. One critic likened Stordahl's string arrangements to a black-velvet cushion setting off a diamond necklace.

In sharp contrast to the garrulous Sinatra, Stordahl was famously closemouthed; musicians joked that Stordahl said two words per session, whether he needed to or not. And unlike his temperamental boss, Stordahl was also that rarity in the

Sinatra does a few impromptu dance steps while rehearsing for a broadcast of Your Hit Parade, *a popular radio show he joined in 1943.*

Jule Styne (left) and Sammy Cahn, two of Sinatra's songwriters.

Astaire had all the great composers of the golden era—among them the Gershwins, Richard Rodgers and Lorenz Hart, and Cole Porter—custom-writing for him. Sinatra sang songs by all these greats, and he also gathered around him a group of songwriters to custom-write songs and whose work fit him like a glove—notably Jule Styne, Sammy Cahn, and Jimmy Van Heusen. Of all these, lyricist Cahn was perhaps Sinatra's perfect match; the singer claimed that "Sammy's words fit my mouth the best."[36]

In addition, however, Sinatra had a gift for unearthing obscure tunes, then recording them simply because he liked them. Because he recorded and kept singing them, these songs became familiar to millions. "She's Funny That Way," "When Your Lover Has Gone," and "Everything Happens to Me" are just three examples.

Sinatra always had an ear for high-quality songs, and he hated having to sing poor ones. Generally he could avoid them, at least during this period in his life, but sometimes it was impossible. For instance, his contract with *Your Hit Parade* stipulated that he had to perform whatever the number one song was that week—which meant he was sometimes saddled with witless material like "Feudin', Fussin' and Fightin'" or "The Too Fat Polka."

Sinatra understood that such lifeless songs don't stand the test of time, and he knew the value of a well-crafted song. He told an interviewer during this period that "an easy song, one that's a novelty, [is] a very short shot that will click right away, but that doesn't last over the years."[37]

music business: a nice guy who kept a steady course under tremendous pressure. Billy May, another talented arranger, once remarked, "People would explode, and Axel would just stand there, lighting and then smoking his pipe. Then, after everybody got their egos out of the way, Axel would go ahead and do his job."[35]

SETTING THE STANDARDS

Sinatra recorded many forgettable songs in his career, but in his prime he recorded a great many that have become classics. In terms of introducing songs to the standard repertoire, Sinatra's only true rival was Fred Astaire.

ON THE SILVER SCREEN

Although singing paid far more, Sinatra was eager to establish himself as an actor. He played himself in his first major screen appearance, 1943's *Higher and Higher*, a cheerfully brainless comedy (with music, of course). In 1944's *Step Lively*, Sinatra was a serious playwright who gets tricked into producing a Broadway musical.

The following year came the first of his memorable pairings with singer and dancer Gene Kelly. *Anchors Aweigh* was one of the biggest hits of the year, a light comedy in which the pair play sailors on shore leave. (Sinatra was so thin that the costumers had to create a false bottom so that he would look normal in his sailor suit.) The two were a natural team and paired up twice more, for *Take Me Out to the Ball Game* and the brilliant *On the Town*.

Sinatra was a Hollywood rookie when he met Kelly, already an established star. The older man taught Sinatra many things, including the basics of dance. "I never worked so goddamned hard in my life," Sinatra said affectionately years later. "Kelly was a brute."[38]

But Kelly also taught the singer a great deal about other things, including acting for the camera and techniques for survival

Gene Kelly (top center) and Sinatra (front right) in a scene from the movie On the Town.

in the volatile world of Hollywood. "He taught me everything I know," Sinatra said. "I couldn't walk, let alone dance. . . . [A]ll of a sudden I was a 'star.' And one of the reasons why I became a 'star' was Gene Kelly."[39]

In these early films, Sinatra comes across as a vulnerable and slightly bewildered innocent. Film critic Robert Horton notes:

He looks like an immigrant kid invited to sit at the same table as the sophisticates: happy, likable, not sure which fork to use. While Gene Kelly grins with the kind of confidence Frankie would have a decade later, The Voice is limited to boyishness and sidekick duties. He's surprisingly non-threatening, considering that he is, for crying out loud, Frank Sinatra.[40]

POLITICS

It was unusual at the time for an entertainer to speak out publicly about politics, and there was a stir when Sinatra re-

---

AN EARLY CRUSADE

In Friedwald's Sinatra: The Song Is You: A Singer's Art, *Bud Granoff, the assistant to Sinatra's press agent George Evans, recalls the beginning of Sinatra's public crusade against intolerance in 1945.*

"George . . . was very political and so was Frank, and in that period he was very liberal in his politics. George was always trying to create the image that Frank was more than just a pop singer, and he had a friend who was a principal at a high school in the Bronx. It was George's idea to get Frank to go and address this high school auditorium and talk to the kids about juvenile delinquency. But Frank said he didn't feel qualified, he didn't feel he could handle it. But George pressured him and pressured him and pressured him, and finally Frank did it, and it wound up on the front page of the *Daily News*.

It was a big front-page story with a picture of Frank talking to these kids. Well, Frank saw the response this brought, so they embarked on a nationwide tour. Frank started to address groups of kids in different cities. I think he did about ten cities, and this got a whirlwind of publicity and sort of changed the image of Frank from being an ordinary record performer, a record star, into a public figure of some importance. In those days performers weren't political activists, but he was one of the first ones."

---

vealed himself as an admirer of Franklin D. Roosevelt. An even bigger stir was caused by a short film Sinatra made during the war, *The House I Live In*.

This movie, which was distributed free to theaters, championed a then-controversial stand: equal rights for all people. In it, Sinatra makes a plea for tolerance to a group of teens:

> Look, fellas, religion makes no difference except to a Nazi or somebody as stupid. My dad came from Italy, but I'm an American. Should I hate your father 'cause he came from Ireland or France or Russia? Wouldn't that make me a first-class fathead?[41]

The film received a special Oscar, but Sinatra's liberal attitudes brought him increasingly under attack from conservatives who suspected him of anti-American leanings. The Federal Bureau of Investigation opened a file on Sinatra, which eventually grew into thirteen hundred pages of gossip, reports, news clippings, and anonymous crackpot letters.

The FBI file never found evidence that Sinatra ever engaged in criminal or anti-American acts. It noted that the singer "has made public appearances and utterances in connection with combating racial and religious intolerance," allegedly "struck a counterman in a cafe down South" who refused to serve a black man in Sinatra's party, knocked down a nightclub patron over an anti-Semitic remark, and was one of the sponsors of an organization called the American Crusade to End Lynchings.

Not all of the FBI's comments regarded politics. In 1945, after an agent reported that teenage girls began lining up at 2 A.M. outside a Detroit theater where Sinatra was to perform, FBI director J. Edgar Hoover sourly commented, "Sinatra is as much to blame as are the moronic bobbysoxers."[42]

HANGING OUT WITH THE TOUGH GUYS

Even in the days of the Rustic Cabin, Sinatra had kept around him a staff and various hangers-on. Sinatra's cohorts, known in the 1940s as the Varsity, could be at times as violence-prone as their boss. And some of the Varsity's friends were known mobsters; violent people had been part of Sinatra's life since childhood, and the singer never seemed to reject the companionship of those who lived outside the law.

Public accusations that Sinatra associated with organized crime figures haunted him all his life. There were those persistent rumors, for instance, about Sinatra's escape from the onerous contract with Tommy Dorsey. Most of the rumors remained rumors.

However, one documented instance of Sinatra's connection to organized crime came in 1947, when he traveled to Cuba with mobster Joe Fischetti to meet the exiled underworld legend Lucky Luciano. Sinatra tried to keep this visit secret, but a journalist saw him in Havana and created an international ruckus.

Testifying later before a Senate committee on organized crime about this trip, Sinatra implacably insisted that he had no

The cover of Frank Sinatra's first hit album, The Voice.

idea who Luciano was, and that the meeting was innocent: "I was brought up to shake a man's hand when introduced to him without first investigating his past."[43]

The uproar over the Havana trip did not deflect Sinatra's popularity. His first number one song under his own name, "Oh, What It Seemed to Be," remained at the top of the charts for eight weeks in 1945. The same year, Sinatra became a pioneer in a new concept: record albums, as opposed to isolated singles. *The Voice,* a collection of 78 rpm records with a special cardboard holder, reached number one and was the first of an eventual seventy-four hit albums for Sinatra.

His recorded output during this period was prodigious. In the years 1946 and 1947 alone, Sinatra recorded 124 studio tracks, not counting miscellaneous material such as alternate takes and radio air checks. He was, by almost any reckoning, the most popular singer in the land. But August 1946 marked his last top ten record until 1954, and harder times were coming. Sinatra was about to plunge to the bottom before he surfaced again.

4 Down and Up Again

You have to scrape bottom to appreciate life and start living again.

—Frank Sinatra

Sinatra had been riding high for most of the 1940s. In the late 1940s and early '50s, however, he experienced a stunning fall—losing virtually everything he had, both personal and professional—and then staged an equally dramatic comeback.

Many factors contributed to his downfall. Simple overwork and stress were greatly to blame; he was a big star, working constantly and sleeping little. Not only was he smoking and drinking heavily, but he had abandoned his regime of swimming and running.

An antagonistic relationship with the press hardly helped, undermining the goodwill Sinatra had earned through benefit performances and other public-spirited actions. At one point, he was voted "Least Cooperative Star" by the Hollywood Women's Press Club. This already poor connection was made even worse by an incident that occurred in the spring of 1947.

A right-wing, gossipy newspaper columnist, Lee Mortimer, had been pestering Sinatra for months, printing unsubstantiated stories about the singer's gangland

(Left to right) Lee Mortimer's attorney, Mortimer, and Sinatra's lawyer look over their settlement.

"SALOONS ARE NOT RUN BY THE CHRISTIAN BROTHERS."

Rumors that Sinatra had dealings with underworld figures dogged him all his adult life. In this excerpt from Hamill's Why Sinatra Matters, *the singer reflects on this.*

"Did I know those guys? Sure, I knew some of those guys. I spent a lot of time working in saloons. And saloons are not run by the Christian Brothers. There were a lot of guys around, and they came out of Prohibition, and they ran pretty good saloons. I was a kid. I worked in the places that were open. They paid you, and the checks didn't bounce. I didn't meet any Nobel Prize winners in saloons. But if Francis of Assisi was a singer and worked in saloons, he would've met the same guys. That doesn't make him part of something. They said hello, you said hello. They came backstage. They thanked you. You offered them a drink. That was it."

connections, implying that he was anti-American, and mocking his music as fit only for "imbecilic, moronic, screaming-meemie autograph kids."[44] When the two met by chance at a Hollywood nightclub, a scuffle ensued and Sinatra knocked the columnist down.

Sinatra claimed that Mortimer had called him "dirty dago," but several impartial witnesses said that was not so. The singer was ordered to publicly apologize and pay $9,000 in settlement costs, which he claimed he was proud to pay. But the real costs to Sinatra were far higher; even though almost no one in the newspaper business seemed to like or respect Mortimer, after the incident many journalists became much tougher on Sinatra than they had been. Much as they disliked Mortimer, he was one of their community; Sinatra was not.

On top of overwork and a bad-tempered relationship with the press came the most significant factor in Sinatra's fall from professional and personal grace. It was a mutually destructive relationship with a woman who was as charismatic, powerful, and willful as the singer himself. "The years from 1949 to 1952 were the most difficult of Sinatra's life," writes biographer Donald Clarke, "and at the center of his problems was a woman, the one person whom he could never dominate. Her name was Ava Gardner."[45]

AVA

One of seven children of a North Carolina tobacco sharecropper, Ava Gardner was already a top movie star when she met Sinatra in 1946. She had already been married to actor Mickey Rooney and bandleader Artie Shaw, and was at the time seeing the multimillionaire entrepreneur Howard Hughes.

She had a reputation for being hard-hearted, hard-drinking, highly sensual, and completely self-absorbed. Within a short time she and Sinatra were embarked on an affair that Broadway columnist Earl Wilson, generally sympathetic to Sinatra, called a "soap opera with screaming fights heard round the world."[46]

Although both Frank and Ava were publicly promiscuous with other partners, each was given, as well, to violent fits of jealousy. Their arguments were frequent, loud, and childish. They often took place in restaurants or nightclubs; frequently, the police had to be called in. Reportedly, Sinatra twice attempted suicide over her.

He could also be cruel and vengeful: Once in New York, after an especially bad argument, Sinatra called Gardner's adjoining suite, said on the phone that he couldn't

Sinatra met movie star Ava Gardner in 1946 and the two soon began a volatile affair.

stand it anymore, and fired a gun. Ava ran into his suite, distraught, and found Frank lying facedown with a gun next to him. When she screamed, Sinatra looked up and coolly said hello; he'd shot the mattress.

Unsurprisingly, the flagrant affair was very painful to Nancy Sinatra, who by now had three young children. Besides her namesake, Nancy, Franklin Emanuel had been born in 1944 (he was named for Franklin D. Roosevelt and his father's best friend, Manie Sachs, but was known then and now as Frank Jr.); Christina, or Tina, was born in 1948.

DIVORCE AND REMARRIAGE

The same year, with Sinatra by now a millionaire several times over, his family moved to a house in the swanky Holmby Hills section of Beverly Hills. Sinatra's publicity people worked hard to project an image of a wholesome family man who loved his home life. Nonetheless, the singer was rarely at home, instead being linked romantically with some of the most glamorous women in the world.

In addition to Gardner, those he dated over the years included actresses Lana Turner, Joan Crawford, Marlene

Frank and Nancy Sinatra and their children (left to right) Nancy, Tina, and Frank Jr. The Sinatras' marriage was marred by Frank's infidelity.

Dietrich, Kim Novak, Angie Dickenson, Eva Gabor, Natalie Wood, Marilyn Monroe, Sophia Loren, Judy Garland, Lauren Bacall, and Juliet Prowse. Sinatra's friend Humphrey Bogart once commented that Sinatra thought paradise would be a place with plenty of women and no newspapermen. "He doesn't realize it," Bogie wryly added, "but he'd be better off if it were the other way around."[47]

When Sinatra brought Gardner with him to a singing engagement in Houston, not even attempting to hide the liaison, his long-suffering wife Nancy finally had enough. On Valentine's Day 1950, she filed for separation and reluctantly granted a divorce in May 1951. When Sinatra divorced, it was a scandal heard around the world; many priests told their parishes not to buy Sinatra records.

The singer remained on good terms with his wife, despite the divorce. As many observers have commented, Sinatra was a dutiful father but a bad husband; he always respected Nancy and often expressed regret that the marriage failed. He was a regular visitor to Nancy's house while their children were growing up, and the two adults generally treated each other with affection. Nancy Sinatra never remarried, often remarking simply, "When you've been married to Sinatra. . . ."

Eight days after the divorce became final in the fall of 1951, Frank and Ava were married. The union lasted less than two years, though the couple would not be formally divorced until 1957.

Sinatra and his second wife Ava Gardner, whom he married in 1951.

"WALKING OFF A CLIFF"

Ava Gardner was not the sole cause of Sinatra's downfall, of course; their mutually self-destructive relationship only compounded other problems.

One manifestation of the singer's grueling work schedule was the toll it took on his voice. During an engagement in 1950 at New York's Copacabana Club, Sinatra opened his mouth and nothing came out. His musical director at the time, Skitch Henderson, remembered the shocked audience: "It became so quiet, so intensely quiet in the club—they were like watching a man walking off a cliff."[48]

Sinatra whispered a mortified "good night," left the stage, and canceled the rest of the gig. His vocal cords had hemorrhaged and he was forced to rest his voice for forty days, not even speaking.

That same year, Sinatra tried his hand at television. The singer had generally resisted the then-new medium, perhaps sensing that radio was his natural home. However, he made an appearance on a special hosted by famed comedian Bob Hope in May 1950, and that fall he began a series of his own.

The series, a sixty-minute variety show, survived two seasons, but it was not a success. There were occasional bright spots—mostly the songs, of course, with their arrangements by Axel Stordahl. But otherwise Sinatra seemed ill at ease, and his lack of natural comic timing was painfully clear on TV. Furthermore, in those days of live television broadcasting, his disdain for rehearsal made him a poor host to his guests and drove his producers crazy. The show was quickly canceled.

Sinatra's movies also fared poorly. After his early films, the singer, always fanatically scrupulous when making recordings, grew increasingly sloppy about his acting. Then, in 1949 Sinatra made a crude remark in the MGM cafeteria about the girlfriend of studio chief Louis B. Mayer. When Mayer got wind of the wisecrack, Sinatra's contract with MGM was suddenly withdrawn.

Sinatra's next movies for other studios, *Double Dynamite* and *Meet Danny Wilson*, were both resounding flops. After that, hewing to the old adage that "you're only as good as your last picture," the Hollywood studios began to ignore Sinatra's calls.

The singer had lost Nancy; his relationship with Ava was rocky; his movie career was dry; his TV show had been canceled; and he couldn't get nightclub contracts because everyone thought his voice was gone. Then, in 1952 his booking agency dropped him, claiming he owed them over $100,000.

"MAMA WILL BARK"

Soon, even Sinatra's recording career—the thing that had first catapulted him to fame—would stall as well.

In the 1940s Columbia Records, the singer's longtime label, had begun introducing a new technology, the long-playing record or LP, with great success. It was quickly becoming the industry standard because of its superior technology—you could play six or seven songs without having to turn the record over!

Unfortunately, Sinatra's first LP, *Sing and Dance with Frank Sinatra*, was a disappointment artistically and financially. Sinatra's voice was so ragged that, for the first time, he was forced to record overdubs. The orchestra was recorded first, and later the singer snuck into the studio (against union rules at the time).

Without an empathetic orchestra for Sinatra to interact with live, the results were predictably poor. Desperate for a hit, Sinatra bowed to Columbia's demands that he work with producer Mitch Miller, a man many fans and scholars consider the worst thing to happen to American pop music in decades.

Miller was a classically trained oboist who had forged a wildly successful career

At his label's request, Sinatra began working with producer Mitch Miller (pictured).

at Columbia—successful financially, that is. He had a knack for producing hit singles that threw in every gimmicky device in the book: banjos, harpsichords, Hawaiian guitars, bagpipes, sing-along choruses, even goofy sound effects. Furthermore, the material he liked was silly throwaway fluff. Aficionados of 1950s pop were deeply dismayed—and still are—to hear gifted singers like Rosemary Clooney and Dinah Shore get the Miller treatment.

Nevertheless, to keep Miller happy and thus avoid losing his contract with Columbia, Sinatra recorded material like "One Finger Melody," "Too Fat Polka," and "Tennessee Newsboy." At the same time as he was recording these lightweight novel-

ties, Sinatra continued to record more suitable material with arrangements by Stordahl and others. This led to some bizarre singles: In 1951, for instance, Sinatra recorded a heartbreaking version of "I'm A Fool to Want You," which many observers feel expresses his anguish over Ava Gardner. The flip side was "Mama Will Bark," a nonsensical duet with a nonsinger named Dagmar that came complete with—yes—dog barks.

"Holiday's Over, Charlie"

In 1952 Sinatra and Columbia parted ways. Accounts vary as to details: He had been unhappy there for some time and had talked of leaving when his contract ran out, but apparently the label dropped him first.

It was a serious blow, the final thing he could lose. Sinatra was at the end of his rope. But the fallow period did not last; the singer spent some time at the bottom and then began to climb back up. As he later remarked:

> I was in trouble. I was busted, and I must say that I lost a great deal of faith in human nature because a lot of friends I had in those days disappeared. I did lie down for a while and had some large bar bills for about a year. [Then] I said "Okay, holiday's over, Charlie. Let's go back to work."[49]

The turnaround came when Sinatra signed late in 1952 with a new agent, Sam Weisbrod, at the William Morris Agency.

In 1953 Sinatra signed with Capitol Records, a small but successful label.

its artists; singers like Nat King Cole, Dinah Shore, and Jo Stafford, Sinatra's former Dorsey bandmate, were making records for Capitol that were both financially successful and artistically satisfying.

Alan Livingston, the head of A&R for Capitol, took a chance that the singer's slump was only temporary. His offer was modest: a standard contract for one year with options for six more years. The singer received no advance, and even had to pay his recording costs. It was a serious comedown from the powerful deals Sinatra had once commanded, but it was a contract nonetheless.

The new arrangement was finalized in the spring of 1953, but most of Livingston's colleagues at Capitol were not as enthusiastic as he was about Sinatra. He remembered later that a collective groan would arise when he would announce to sales teams and other Capitol groups that the label had just signed Sinatra. The consensus was that he was a genuine has-been—a washed-up singer with a ruined voice.

ENTER NELSON RIDDLE

Shortly after signing his contract, Sinatra recorded his first sides for Capitol, with Axel Stordahl arranging. One song, "I'm Walking Behind You," was a modest hit. But then Stordahl took a job with singer Eddie Fisher, and Sinatra's next choice, Billy May, was also unavailable. Someone at Capitol—accounts vary, but it was either Livingston or producer Voyle Gilmore—then hooked him up with an arranger named Nelson Riddle.

Weisbrod approached a small label, Capitol Records, about signing Sinatra. Capitol was one of the few record labels of any size based on the West Coast, but it was thriving and had a reputation for being sensitive to

It was a felicitous choice and a perfect match. Biographer Donald Clarke does not exaggerate when he calls the pairing of singer and arranger "one of the greatest teams in the history of popular music."[50]

Riddle, who would eventually work on over three hundred Sinatra recordings, was already a seasoned pro. He had worked for Tommy Dorsey and for years had been Nat King Cole's musical director. It was Riddle who had created the sublime string arrangement that had helped make Cole's "Mona Lisa" into a huge hit and an enduring standard.

In their first session together, Sinatra and Riddle recorded eight songs. Listening to the playbacks, Sinatra was ecstatic; he loved the sound Riddle had created, and he loved the material. He walked around the studio afterward, slapping musicians on the back and jubilantly saying that he was on his way back. Sure enough, three of the songs, including the tellingly titled "I've Got the World on a String," made it into the top twenty.

The sound was indeed very different from anything else Sinatra had ever done, not just the arrangements and material but Sinatra's voice as well. His trademark fragility was gone, replaced by a confident, mature sense; this, listeners sensed, was a grown man who understood both joy and sadness. Nelson Riddle felt that the great passion and great loss of Sinatra's life was the reason for the change: "It was Ava who did that, who taught him how to sing a torch song. . . . She was the great love of his life and he lost her."[51]

MAGGIO

Sinatra's film career was about to bounce back as well. Columbia Pictures (no relation to the record company) had bought the film rights to James Jones's best-selling World War II epic *From Here to Eternity*, and Sinatra was determined to play the supporting role of Maggio, a wisecracking Italian American GI. The singer was confident he fit the bill: "I knew Maggio. I grew up with him in Hoboken."[52]

Sinatra approached the studio head, Harry Cohn, about it. Ava Gardner did her part as well, despite her troubled relationship with the singer; she urged Cohn's wife, a close friend, to recommend Sinatra. Sinatra then begged one of the film's producers, Buddy Adler, to give him a screen test, offering to do the film for $8,000 instead of the $150,000 or so he had once commanded for a picture.

Late in 1952, while with Gardner in Africa on location for a film, Sinatra received a telegram offering him the screen test. Thirty-six hours later, he was at the Columbia lot; he was broke, so Ava paid for his plane ticket. But he did not need a script because he had already memorized the part.

According to every source, Sinatra's screen test was amazing, but nonetheless he was not the producers' first choice. They preferred stage actor Eli Wallach, who had never made a movie. But then Wallach decided to do a new Tennessee Williams play on Broadway, and Sinatra got the job.

The shooting for *Eternity* took place at roughly the same time as Sinatra's first recordings with Nelson Riddle, and the singer sensed he was doing excellent work in both. He could not anticipate how successful the film would be, however. It opened in the summer of 1953 and experienced record-breaking business; there was immediate talk of an Oscar for Sinatra's intense performance. Typical of the critical reaction was the review in the *New York Post*: "Instead of exploiting a personality, he proves he is an actor by playing the luckless Maggio with a kind of doomed gaiety that is both real and immensely touching."[53]

BACK AT WORK

The talk of Sinatra's performance being Oscar-worthy was not idle. *From Here to Eternity* was nominated for twelve Academy Awards and won eight of them—the most given to a single film since *Gone with the Wind*. The wins included Best Picture, Best Director, Best Screenplay, and two Best Supporting Performance awards, for Donna Reed and for Frank Sinatra. At the awards ceremony, Sinatra received the longest standing ovation of the evening; he has since commented many times that it was one of the happiest moments of his life.

THE TOUGH MONKEY

Film critic Robert Horton, in his Film Comment *article "One Good Take: Sinatra, 1915–1998," has this to say about the movie role that helped bring about Sinatra's dramatic comeback from the bottom.*

"When his movies fizzled at the box office and his singing career was seriously slowed, Sinatra made his famous comeback with *From Here to Eternity*. . . . The story of Sinatra's resurgence is so captivating that it seems churlish to suggest his performance is less than great, but he relies a bit too much on a Dean Martin–style drunk routine, and does some of the comic relief as though he knew he was providing comic relief. But you love him. He's so slim, so wiry and juiced up; when he's supposed to be insolent, he really looks insolent, and when he's supposed to be excited, he's on the moon. Marching into the stockade, straight as an arrow with plenty of lip, he finally grows into his screen persona: he needed the tough monkey Maggio to bring the chip out onto his shoulder, where it would remain."

Sinatra as Maggio in From Here to Eternity, *a role for which he received a Best Supporting Performance award and a standing ovation at the 1954 Oscars.*

Ava Gardner was also nominated that year for an Oscar, for her role in *Mogambo*, the film she had been shooting in Africa. She did not attend the ceremony with Sinatra; by then, Sinatra had moved out of their home and was sharing a bachelor pad with his longtime friend songwriter Jule Styne. Nonetheless, his life, the singer later commented, was back on track: "I changed record companies, changed attorneys, changed accountants, changed picture companies and changed my clothes. And I just went back to work again."[54]

Sinatra followed up his double-whammy success in recording and the movies with a series of sold-out singing engagements, a string of guest appearances on top TV shows, and a television special of his own. He was, indeed, back at work, and the next decade would be one of his most fulfilling and productive.

Chapter

5 The Classic Years

Sinatra's tempo is the tempo of the heartbeat.

—arranger Nelson Riddle

The period following Sinatra's comeback is considered by most fans and critics to be the golden age of Sinatra.

It was the era that saw the creation of a brilliant string of albums, recorded in collaboration with three gifted arrangers: Nelson Riddle, Billy May, and Gordon Jenkins. These albums are considered by virtually every Sinatra fan to be the crown jewels of Sinatra's career. In Donald Clarke's opinion, "It is not too much to say that Sinatra's enduring reputation as the greatest pop singer of the century could rest on [just his] 1954–57 albums."[55]

Several factors joined together to produce this extraordinary set of recordings. One was simply that Sinatra's voice was in its prime, deepening and drawing from an ever-wider and maturing rhythmic and emotional palette.

Another was the painstaking care the singer took in assembling each album, carefully considering such factors as crescendos and tempos for both indi-

vidual songs and entire LPs. He also paid close attention to creating a theme for each album; they are not simply collections of individual, unrelated songs. Instead, each is a self-contained work exploring such themes as love, loneliness, swinging times, or maturity. Because of this cohesiveness, they are perhaps the first examples of something that has become commonplace in later years: the concept album.

A third factor was the singer's near-perfect taste in choosing material that suited his style; he was his own boss again, and (at least for a while) there would be no more songs like "Mama Will Bark." Finally, a fourth factor was Sinatra's nearly obsessive perfectionism.

He might be sloppy on a movie set, insisting that he do only one take of a scene; but in the recording studio, the singer often insisted on twenty or more takes, with a full orchestra accompanying him each time, before he was satisfied. He once explained, "Somewhere in my subconscious there's the constant alarm that rings, telling me what we're putting on tape might be around for a lotta, lotta years."[56]

RIDDLE

But the biggest single factor in the quality of Sinatra's output during this period was undoubtedly his partnership with Nelson Riddle. Sinatra worked with many other accomplished arrangers over the years, but none meshed with him so perfectly. In journalist Pete Hamill's opinion, the sound they made together was "the mature sound of Frank Sinatra, the sound of the Comeback, the sound of the years when Sinatra always wore a hat and truly seemed to have the world on a string."[57]

Arranging is the art of writing out the parts to be played by each instrument in an orchestra or band (in this case, to back up a singer). Creating such arrangements, called "writing charts," is a highly specialized skill and one of the most underappreciated jobs in the music industry. In the 1950s, at least, it was also scandalously underpaid.

Even a top professional like Riddle in his prime was paid only about $150 per chart, with no royalties.

Since Riddle had six children, an expensive house in Bel Air, and both an ex- and a current wife, he needed to work constantly, not just for Sinatra but for anyone who paid him. A melancholy man with a dry wit, he once said that Sinatra's album *Only the Lonely* was the best work he ever did because he had the luxury of having an entire week to work on it.

Riddle was a former big band trombonist, and his arrangements show a particular affinity for that instrument. This may be one reason why his style suited Sinatra's so well. One of Sinatra's deepest influences had been trombonist Tommy Dorsey, and the instrument itself closely resembles the human voice, in that its notes "slide" from one to another, rather than being discrete

---

FIVE JACKPOTS

In this excerpt from Will Friedwald's Sinatra: The Song Is You: A Singer's Art, *arranger/composer Neal Hefti comments on the string of brilliant collaborations Sinatra and arranger Nelson Riddle made for Capitol Records:*

"It was as if you went to Vegas and hit five jackpots in a row. As far as I'm concerned, no one has even come close to what Nelson achieved with Sinatra. This isn't taking anything away from any of the other people. It's just that the moon and the stars were in the right position at the same time, with Frank and Nelson, plus Capitol Records, plus Frank being so exuberant because he had won the Academy Award. It was all of these things. God! That enthusiasm just keeps going on and on and on! It's just like the Richter scale: each new thing makes the last number ten times higher. It was just unbelievable."

Sinatra (right) teamed up with arranger Nelson Riddle (left) to create some of the singer's most beloved music, launching his so-called "golden age."

stepping-stones like a piano's keys. Nearly from the beginning of his career, Sinatra's style had been trombonelike; he always let his voice slide, unlike more classically "pure" singers, taking his time before hitting the proper note.

Furthermore, Riddle's understated but inventive arrangements always put Sinatra in the best possible light. Arranger/producer Quincy Jones, who worked with the singer in later years, has remarked on Riddle's ability to build arrangements in high registers that set off Sinatra's deepening, burnished voice: "Nelson was smart because he put the electricity up above Frank. He put it way upstairs and gave Frank the room downstairs for his voice to shine, rather than building big lush parts that were in the same register as his voice."[58]

THE CLASSIC ALBUMS

The Sinatra-Riddle albums began with two ten-inch EPs (extended play records, each with four songs per side). *Songs for*

Young Lovers was mostly ballads, scored for a spare "chamber group" of two horns, a rhythm section, and string quartet; the more up-tempo *Swing Easy* featured a tightly swinging fourteen-piece band. Released in 1954, both EPs reached number three on the *Billboard* chart (and were later reissued as a single album). Their success was confirmed when that same year Sinatra topped the *Metronome* and *Down Beat* magazine polls, and *Billboard* named him top male vocalist and *Swing Easy* best album.

The following year came *In the Wee Small Hours*, a collection of songs about unrequited love and loneliness. They reflected, of course, Sinatra's grief over Ava Gardner, but they also evoked Sinatra's unshakable confidence that he would survive. Journalist Pete Hamill writes:

The songs from *In the Wee Small Hours* said that in spite of loss, abandonment, defeat, he—and you—could get through the night. You could still get hurt, but it was worth the risk because you knew that no defeat was permanent. There would be another day, another woman, another chance to roll the dice.[59]

Two albums date from 1956: *Close to You*, a collection of intimate love songs, and the up-tempo *Songs for Swingin' Lovers!* The release and sales of *Songs for Swingin' Lovers!* demonstrate how swiftly Sinatra records could sell: recorded in January and February of '56, it was topping the charts by March. On it is one of the most famous single recordings Sinatra ever made: his version of Cole Porter's "I've Got You Under My Skin," which features an arrangement

By the mid-1950s, Sinatra (center) was at the height of success again, turning out several chart-topping albums.

CRYPTIC LITTLE NOTES

In Hamill's Why Sinatra Matters, *Nelson Riddle and Sinatra reflect on why they admire each other's work:*

"Riddle: Frank and I both have, I think, the same musical aim. We know what we're each doing with a song, what we want the song to say. The way we'd work is this: he'd pick out all the songs for an album and then call me over to go through them. He'd have very definite ideas about the general treatment, particularly about the pace of the record and which areas should be soft or loud, happy or sad.

He'd sketch out something brief, like, 'Start with a bass figure, build up second time through and then fade out at the end.' That's possibly all he would say. Sometimes he'd follow up with a phone call at three in the morning with some other extra little idea. But after that he wouldn't hear my arrangement until the recording session."

"Sinatra: Nothing ever ruffles him. There's a great depth somehow to the music he creates. And he's got a sort of stenographer's brain. If I say to him at a planning meeting, 'Make the eighth bar sound like Brahms,' he'll make a cryptic little note on the side of some crappy music sheet and, sure enough, when we come to the session the eighth bar will be Brahms. If I say, 'Make like Puccini,' Nelson will make exactly the same little note and that eighth bar will be Puccini all right, and the roof will lift off."

so sublime that when they finished rehearsing it, the jaded studio musicians in the orchestra did something virtually unheard of: they stood and applauded for Riddle.

SOLD ONLY BY PRESCRIPTION

The singer released two albums in 1957: the lean and punchy *A Swingin' Affair* and the tender *Where Are You?* Several more albums complete the classic Capitol-years cycle, including *Nice 'n' Easy* (1960) and *Sinatra's Swingin' Session* (1961).

But it was a 1958 album that many Sinatra connoisseurs consider his masterpiece, the magnificently sad *Only the Lonely*. Sinatra's son once described the album's late-night melancholy as so devastating that it "should be available in drugstores by prescription only—because this is death, this record."[60]

The album was recorded soon after the singer's traumatic breakup with a girlfriend, and its dark undertones certainly reflect his shattered love life. Nelson Riddle had recently had sorrows of his own, which might also have affected the album's mood: his mother had died of cancer a few weeks before, and his infant daughter had died only three months earlier.

Only the Lonely goes further than recent sorrows, however. It seems to distill decades of loneliness and yearning, emotions that go far beyond a single love affair. As Pete Hamill has noted, such deep loneliness was, in essence, the singer's great subject: "As an artist, Sinatra had only one basic subject: loneliness. His ballads are all strategies for dealing with loneliness; his up-tempo performances are expressions of release from that loneliness."[61]

The album's pinnacle—or lowest depth, depending on the point of view—is "One for My Baby," a poignant ballad that forever after became identified as Sinatra's quintessential "saloon song." Music historian Will Friedwald writes of its understated power:

> "One for My Baby" is the finest piece of musical acting Sinatra has ever turned in. He has never sounded closer to the end of his rope, and he makes the lyric come alive, word by painful word, in an intimate reality that's as frightening as it is believable.[62]

Sinatra expressed his sorrow and loneliness in Only the Lonely, *an album many consider his best work.*

WITHOUT RIDDLE

After working with Riddle on ten albums, Sinatra decided to branch out. The Sinatra-Riddle sound was undeniably popular; between February 1954 and May 1957, every one of Sinatra's first seven LPs for Capitol reached the top ten

"As Close as You're Gonna Get"

Sinatra worked often with arranger Gordon Jenkins. Here, Jenkins reflects on the magic that took place during their collaborations. The quote is from Friedwald's Sinatra: The Song Is You: A Singer's Art.

"It's as close as you're gonna get without being [of the] opposite sex. Because I like to have him right in front of me, and I just never take my eyes off him. It's kind of a hard thing to describe, but [there's] a definite mental connection between the two of us when it's going down well. He lets it loose. He's all over the place when he's going. He doesn't hold anything back.

But the excitement with [Frank] is following him because he likes to wander around. He doesn't necessarily do a song the way he rehearsed it. So you have to never take your eyes off him. I wouldn't dare. You have to just never let up or relax for a minute. . . . He might give you a little hint, but he might not, and he assumes you'll be there.

Frank is withdrawn. He's the charmer of all time when he feels like being charming. Nobody comes close to him. But when he quits laughing, you're not any closer to him than you were before. You talk about high standards— he's the inventor! The things that he's gotten into, scrapes and bad publicity, in my opinion are only because he expected more of people than they ever delivered. If he hires you to do something, he expects it to be the absolute world's best, whether it's cutting the grass or playing the piano. He never questions how much money—he pays whatever you want, really—but he expects it to be absolutely perfect. And it depresses him when it isn't.

Also, I stay away from him as much as I can when we're not working. It's a temptation to hang around him because he has so much to offer, but I figure that we've gotten along fine by not being buddies. So when we get through at night, if he goes out the left door, I go out the right door. I think it's worked out fine."

charts, and only one, a compilation of singles, did not crack the top five. One Sinatra album from this period, *Only the Lonely*, remained on the charts for 120 weeks; another, *Come Dance with Me*, lasted for 140 weeks. One measure of the singer's popularity was his appearance on the cover of *Time* magazine in 1957 as the highest paid entertainer in the history of show business.

But Sinatra was wary of falling into a rut, and he wanted to find a different sound. There may have been another factor in his decision: there were rumors at the time that he was jealous of the increasing amount of credit Riddle was getting for their successful sound.

Though Sinatra continued to work with Riddle, Gordon Jenkins and Billy May became regular replacements. Jenkins specialized in a lush, string-laden sound, and Sinatra employed him for ballad-heavy albums like *Where Are You?*, *No One Cares*, and *All Alone*. A very different ambience was provided by Billy May, whose brash, brass-heavy, swinging style Sinatra often compared to a glassful of cold water in the face. May came on board for such up-tempo albums as *Come Fly with Me*, *Come Dance with Me*, and *Come Swing with Me*.

Though he could barely read sheet music, the singer had a sharp sense for conducting. In addition to his own records, he recorded a handful of albums with himself at the baton during this period, including sessions for Peggy Lee and Dean Martin and an all-instrumental album called *Tone Poems of Color*.

REPRISE

In the late 1950s the singer began negotiating a release from his contract with Capitol, which he felt was taking advantage of him financially. The dispute was not settled until early 1960, and toward the end the disagreement between singer and label affected the quality of his work. Sinatra later remarked, "You can't give your best when you're not happy with the people you're [working] for. I wasn't happy with Capitol, and I'm afraid some of those later albums show it."[63]

Once free of his contract, Sinatra knew what he wanted: his own record label. He quickly hired a number of music business veterans to help him. One day the singer was driving with Mo Ostin, the newly appointed president of his record company, past the Capitol Records Tower in Los Angeles; Sinatra pointed and said, "I helped build that. Now let's build one of our own."[64]

The new label was called Reprise, a word that normally rhymes with "re-freeze." Sinatra, however, always pronounced it "re-prize," as in "reprisal," and more than one observer has surmised that Sinatra founded the label at least in part as a way to get back at Capitol Records. (Capitol got its own revenge by flooding the market with repackaged older Sinatra material on sale at bargain prices.)

Reprise's first releases included albums by former Ellington saxophonist Ben Webster and singer Sammy Davis Jr. They were soon joined by an all-star roster including Dean Martin, Bing Crosby, Rosemary Clooney, and Duke Ellington.

Sinatra (right) worked on arrangements with jazz musician Count Basie (left) and toured with the Count Basie Orchestra in the early 1960s.

The label appealed to musicians because Sinatra understood and respected their needs. He guaranteed that all artists would retain ownership of their own master recordings, issued them shares in the company stock, and did not require them to sign exclusive contracts.

MORE SINATRA

Needless to say, there were also Sinatra records on Reprise.

Ring-a-Ding-Ding, arranged by Johnny Mandel, was the first in a series of "one-shot" albums the singer recorded, each with a different arranger. Others included *I Remember Tommy* (a Dorsey tribute album) with Sy Oliver; *Point of No Return* with Axel Stordahl (that arranger's last work; he died of cancer shortly after its completion); *Sinatra and Strings* with Don Costa;

Sinatra and Swingin' Brass and *Sinatra-Basie*, both with arrangements by Neal Hefti; *It Might as Well Be Swing*, with the Count Basie Orchestra and arrangements by Quincy Jones; and *Francis Albert Sinatra–Antonio Carlos Jobim*, with arrangements by Claus Ogerman.

In 1963 Sinatra formed an offbeat side project. The Reprise Repertory Group was a loose affiliation of singers that included himself, Martin, Crosby, Clooney, Davis, Jo Stafford, and the McGuire Sisters. The group recorded four albums re-creating hit Broadway shows: *Finian's Rainbow, Kiss Me Kate, South Pacific*, and *Guys and Dolls*.

With mixed results, Sinatra also collaborated with two of jazz's greatest figures: Duke Ellington and Count Basie.

Legendary bandleader Duke Ellington had spent decades assembling an orchestra that could brilliantly perform his own compositions and arrangements. But their skills were largely wasted on *Francis A. and Edward K.*; the arrangements were not by the incomparable Duke but by Billy May, and the Ellington band played them only halfheartedly. Compounding the problem was the fact that Sinatra's voice, through overwork, was not at its peak.

Sinatra-Basie paired the singer with another giant of American music. But the material was uninspired, and Sinatra's throat was again in poor shape; he had strained his voice yelling at TV broadcasts of his beloved Dodgers in the World Series. Later albums with Basie (*It Might as Well Be Swing* and *Sinatra at the Sands*) were more successful. At least the two celebrities got along well, Frank Foster, Basie's longtime lead tenor saxophonist, recalled: "Basie and Frank always seemed to have a great relationship going on. I know Sinatra always talks about being a saloon singer. . . . And I imagine Basie hit a few saloons with him."[65]

AT THE MOVIES

Sinatra's Hollywood career during this period remained at an average of about two movies a year plus brief cameo appearances. Unfortunately, it was in general more uneven than his recordings.

His most consistently successful films were musicals, still a popular form of movie. The best of these include *Young at Heart* with Doris Day; *Pal Joey*, with its superior score by Rodgers and Hart; *Can-Can*, costarring veteran French entertainer Maurice Chevalier and Sinatra's pal Shirley MacLaine; and *High Society*,

with Bing Crosby, Louis Armstrong, and Grace Kelly.

One of the best of these musicals was *Guys and Dolls*, the film version of Frank Loesser's hit musical about lovable crooks and gamblers. The movie is enjoyable despite having been seriously miscast: Marlon Brando, who had a sweet but very slight singing voice, was given the role with all the good songs!

As a dramatic actor, Sinatra performed in such varied material as a thriller, *Suddenly*; a hospital drama, *Not as a Stranger*; an elaborate costume drama, *The Pride and the Passion*; and a romantic comedy, *The Tender Trap*. Two of his performances stand out for their intensity and emotional power. In *The Manchurian Candidate*, Sinatra portrays an ex-soldier caught up in a

Sinatra (left) and Bing Crosby in the musical High Society.

complex political intrigue. In *The Man with the Golden Arm*, Sinatra is Frankie Machine, a heroin-addicted card dealer and would-be musician.

Sinatra was, in general, notoriously difficult on a movie set: rude, impossible to please, and contemptuous. When the shooting schedule for *Some Came Running* fell behind, Sinatra tore twenty pages out of his copy of the script, handed it to an assistant director, and announced that *now* things were on schedule. Such behavior was in sharp contrast to his perfectionist attitude in the recording studio, where he was always friendly and respectful toward musicians. Sinatra simply refused to take acting as seriously as singing.

On TV

The singer also gamely took a few tries at television again. His role as the stage manager in a TV musical production of the play *Our Town* was a critical and artistic success; his final attempt at a variety series, in 1957, was so disastrous that it moved veteran director Jack Donohue to comment, "There are quite a few performers who have no business on television each week, and Sinatra is one of them."[66]

Although he had artistic control and majority ownership of the shows, Sinatra seemed to do everything possible to undermine them. His disdain for preparation ruined the tight schedules necessary for producing live shows. He never learned his lines, instead reading them from a prompter. Worst of all, his on-screen manner was stiff and wooden.

The ratings were terrible, and after only a handful of shows, the singer's contract was canceled.

In 1960 Sinatra hosted a handful of hour-long specials for ABC, in an attempt to recoup the money lost on his disastrous series. On one of these, Frank Sinatra and Elvis Presley—two singers so popular

Elvis Presley (right) and Sinatra in their 1960 TV appearance.

they had sparked riots and had become the foremost musical icons of their generations—met for the first time.

Eager to earn high ratings for his show, Sinatra agreed to welcome Elvis in the rocker's first public appearance after his stint in the army. Elvis sang one of Sinatra's signature tunes, "Witchcraft," and together they sang "Love Me Tender," a nineteenth-century campfire song that both singers had turned into hit records. It was a thrill for Elvis, who had idolized Sinatra's friend Dean Martin, and also for Sinatra, who disliked Presley but got the high ratings he had sought.

A WEALTHY MAN

Artistically, the singer's golden age was a smash success. Financially it was also rewarding, and Sinatra became even wealthier than before.

Reprise Records was extremely profitable, and it was only part of Sinatra's financial empire. The singer also various times, pieces of such varied ests as a charter airline, a missile pa company, a music publishing house, radi stations, restaurants, real estate, production companies for both movies and recordings, and Nevada gambling casinos. At its height, the Sinatra financial empire employed about a hundred people, and his personal wealth eventually grew to an estimated $200 million.

This wealth was only one aspect of Sinatra's power within the entertainment industry. The era during which he produced his classic recordings—roughly the mid-1950s to the mid-1960s—were also Sinatra's prime years of power, fame, and controversy. He was the center of a circle of friends who ruled the entertainment world, with connections reaching as far up as the White House and as far down as the centers of the organized crime underworld. These were the years when Sinatra became known as the Chairman of the Board.

he Chairman of the Board

It's Frank's world—we just live in it.

—allegedly first said by Dean Martin, popular as a lapel pin slogan during the Rat Pack years

The years when Sinatra was king of the hill in pop music, one of the highest-paid and best-known entertainers in the world, was the era that produced what was probably the singer's most famous image. The hat, the raincoat slung over the shoulder, the sharp suit and thin tie, the cigarette and whiskey glass in hand—all came together to form a powerful, lasting image of cool confidence, swinging '60s style.

But Sinatra was far more than just a sharp fashion plate. He used his celebrity to gain access and power in a wide variety of settings, assuming in each a leadership role that inspired disc jockey William B. Williams to dub the singer "the Chairman of the Board."

THE TRAPPINGS OF POWER

Sinatra certainly enjoyed the trappings of power. He liked showy entrances and exits, such as insisting on a police escort whenever he left Vegas—even if it was four in the morning. There were also frequent occasions of violence, although the singer relied less and less on his own fighting skills, preferring instead to order one of his burly friends or employees to do the job.

Perhaps the most flamboyant of all the trappings of power was Sinatra's habit, one he had enjoyed since his days in Hoboken, of making grand gestures of generosity. These gestures, according to many observers, were the only way the singer could show affection.

Over and over, Sinatra lavished gifts of money and time, even on relative strangers. He covered the bills when financially strapped actor Lee J. Cobb suffered a heart attack, when singer/dancer Sammy Davis Jr. lost an eye in a car accident, when the owner of the El Mocambo nightclub died suddenly with big debts and no insurance for his family, and when prizefighter Joe Louis suffered a stroke.

After a mud slide destroyed the home of Sinatra's pianist Bill Miller, killing Miller's wife and seriously injuring the piano player, the singer bought Miller a new house and paid his medical bills. When actor George Raft, whose days as a high-earning star were over, came under indictment for income tax evasion, Sinatra sent him a blank check with a note saying it was to be used as needed.

And when comedian Phil Silvers's longtime partner Rags Ragland died suddenly, Sinatra dropped everything and flew cross-country to finish an engagement with the grief-stricken Silvers. Sinatra knew all of Ragland's lines already, since he and Silvers had appeared in USO shows together during the war.

TWO GUYS

Even when there was no crisis, Sinatra loved to lavish gifts on his friends. Typical were chartered yachts and rides in his three jets; expensive instruments for musicians he liked, such as a $5,000 guitar for his accompanist Al Viola; and paid-for hotel bills, cars, gambling tabs, and jewelry for attractive women.

He was most attentive to guests in his home, personally stocking their bathrooms with expensive soaps and the like. Actress Rosalind Russell described him once as "a knitter-together of people, a constant plate-filler and glass-replenisher."[67] It was during these years that friends began to call him the Innkeeper.

For all of his famed foul mouth and short temper, Sinatra was also unfailingly chivalrous toward women, and he insisted that everyone in his company be the same way. He did not tolerate bad language around (or by) women, and he did not approve of public lechery. Double-entendre jokes onstage were acceptable, but not outright crudity.

Those who made a mistake regarding chivalry in the singer's presence did it only once. At a celebrity roast dinner in 1977, Sinatra's old friend Gene Kelly joked, "He was a special kind of guy and very generous. If you admired his tie, he'd send you a tie just like it. If you said, 'I like your suit,' Frank would send you a suit. If you said, 'I like your girl,' he'd send over two guys named Carmine and Nunzio."[68]

Sinatra (left) and Phil Silvers at the Copacabana nightclub in New York City.

Loyalty

Sinatra's generosity sometimes involved not money but his own time and attention. This philanthropy could sometimes be overwhelming.

His friends sometimes avoided telling the singer their troubles, because he immediately assumed them as his own; solving the problems of others was another way Sinatra could exercise his power. Actor Burt Lancaster, Sinatra's costar in *From Here to Eternity*, once remarked of his friend, "You sometimes feel like you have to run away from him, because if you say to Frank, 'I'm having a problem,' it becomes *his* problem. And sometimes maybe you'd rather try to work it out yourself."[69]

The flip side of Sinatra's generosity and attention was that he demanded complete and utter loyalty from his friends. A real or imagined slight could be enough to cause Sinatra to drop someone completely. Many Sinatra observers have remarked on the singer's extreme touchiness. Being sensitive to every nuance of feeling served him brilliantly onstage, they point out, but it was disastrous in his private life; he was constantly overreacting to real or imagined insults and humiliations.

Sinatra and actress Lauren Bacall, whom he began dating after his divorce from Ava Gardner.

There are dozens of examples of this hypersensitivity. After his divorce from Ava Gardner, Sinatra began dating actress Lauren Bacall, the widow of his friend Humphrey Bogart. In the spring of 1958 the couple was secretly engaged, but a friend, theatrical agent Irving "Swifty" Lazar, broke confidence and told the press. Sinatra immediately and very publicly dumped Bacall, and he did not speak to either Bacall or Lazar for years.

In the late '50s, comedian Phil Silvers's television network decided to put Silvers's show on opposite Sinatra's. Sinatra took the move as a personal insult; once a close friend of Silvers's, he did not speak to the comedian for sixteen years.

THE RAT PACK

All his life, Sinatra craved having large groups around him, both friends and "associates" on his payroll. The best known of these groups, which came together in the late 1950s, was a genuine show business phenomenon: the Rat Pack. With Sinatra at its center and Las Vegas as its base, this group of entertainers caused a sensation every time they appeared together, and during its brief life the Rat Pack became a potent force in the era's popular entertainment and culture.

From today's perspective, the Rat Pack can be seen as exemplifying the worst of Vegas-style excess: the boozing, the chain-smoking, the in-jokes, the sexism. But to many at the time, the Pack was the ultimate in hip. The bad boys of the entertainment world, they were a blast of fresh air after the stifling conventions of the

Rat Pack members (clockwise from left) Sinatra, Martin, Lawford, Bishop, and Davis.

postwar '50s. The press and public alike couldn't get enough of the Rat Pack, even as they deplored its worst traits.

The Rat Pack's fashion style, iconoclastic attitude, and rude humor were widely imitated. Even its slang became a part of every fan's jargon. A good guy was a Charlie; a jerk was a Harvey. Women were broads or chicks. "Clyde" was an all-purpose word, as in "Pass the clyde." "Ring-a-ding-ding" was a phrase Sinatra immortalized in a 1961 song of the same name; it was a nonsense phrase that conveyed exhilaration, and some said it symbolized the sound of money falling or telephones ringing with new offers.

THE CORE RAT PACKERS

Many people came and went on the group's fringes—especially a parade of beautiful women—but the core, including Sinatra, numbered five. In an environment still blighted by racism, the Pack—two Italian Catholics, a Jew, an aristocratic Briton, and a black man who had converted to Judaism—was a microcosm of racial and ethnic tolerance.

Dean Martin, born Dino Crocetti, had risen to fame as part of a team with comedian Jerry Lewis; before a bitter breakup in 1958, they had formed one of the country's top nightclub acts and starred in several very successful and funny movies. A brilliant natural wit, Martin was also a pleasing singer with a cool nonchalance and an easygoing style.

Joey Bishop, born Joseph Gottlieb, was nicknamed the Frown Prince of Comedy for his sad-sack comic delivery. He wrote most of the comedy material used by the Rat Pack, and his acerbic wit was a good fit for the irreverent group.

Suave British actor Peter Lawford, once a leading man but by the mid-1950s something of a has-been, made up for his lack of star power by having married well; his wife's brother was John F. Kennedy, then an up-and-coming senator from Massachusetts who was also a close friend of Sinatra's.

Sammy Davis Jr., a gifted singer/dancer, labored for years on the black entertainment circuit without achieving widespread fame. However, with Sinatra's help, Davis was able to become one of the most famous African American entertainers in the country. Until he and singer Harry Belafonte began performing there in the late 1950s, black entertainers in Las Vegas were not allowed to gamble or otherwise mingle with the white guests of the casinos; they were forced to wait in their hotel rooms until it was time to perform. Davis was a pioneer in breaking down such racial barriers.

SUCH NUTTINESS

World headquarters for the Rat Pack was the Sands Casino in Las Vegas, which they used like a private boys' club. It was a nonstop party when they were in town, as Peter Lawford remembers:

> Everybody was on the same wavelength. We would do two shows a night, get to bed around five, get up again at seven or eight, and go to work on a movie. We'd come back, go to the steam room, get something to eat and start all over again—two shows a night. They were taking bets we'd all end up in a box.[70]

The Pack played to capacity crowds in the casino's Copa Room. Twice each evening, the five pals put on shows that became legends of boozy, irreverent, and wildly unpredictable entertainment. Every night was different—a hodgepodge that usually included singing by Martin, Davis, and Sinatra; dance numbers by Davis and Lawford; comedy skits involving everyone; and seemingly improvised hijinks that were actually scripted and directed by Bishop.

BECOMING FRIENDS

In this excerpt from "The Frank Sinatra I Know," an article he wrote for Down Beat *in August 1956, Sammy Davis Jr. talks about his friend and mentor. The article was reprinted in* Down Beat, *August 1998.*

"I first met Frank Sinatra [in 1942] about three months before he left Tommy Dorsey to go out as a single. The band was playing Detroit, and a unit called Tip, Tap and Toe was to open with them, but the unit was hung up in Canada. So they put us in for three days on the same bill as the band....

[A year later] we met, he said he was going into the Capitol Theater. I told him it would be great for us to get that kind of date. He said, 'Yuh.' Without our knowing it, he went on to pitch us to Sid Piermont, head of Loew's booking agency....

After that, we became very close. I used to go to his home in California, and he'd ask how my career was going. I'd see him about once every six months. This was in the late '40s and early '50s. I was getting a hold in the business. Every time I saw him it was a real breath of spring. No matter which of his own troubles and problems he was involved with then, he always had time to talk to me about my career. He'd advise me what to do and whom to watch out for.... Our friendship has progressed beautifully since then as we've become more and more close."

Sammy Davis Jr. clowns around with friend and colleague Sinatra.

The performing strengths of the individual Rat Packers complemented each other well. For instance, Sinatra was a terrible comedian; he had to strain to get a laugh from an audience, while a natural wit like Martin could crack up a crowd with just a raised eyebrow. Their onstage personalities also balanced one another, according to writer Shawn Levy: "Frank was *cool* in the sense of *remote*. Dean and Sammy were *warm* in the sense of *comfortable*."[71]

Drinking onstage was an integral part of the Rat Pack image, long before such casual behavior became common, and they made it into a romantic, sexy asset to their performances. The Jack Daniel's whiskey company once presented Sinatra with an acre of Tennessee land in recognition of his role as a one-man unpaid ad campaign for their product.

The performances were very loosely structured. The entertainers might wander off into the wings midroutine, go into the audience and heckle those who were onstage, perform wicked impressions of each other, or pour drinks from a bar cart kept onstage. Sammy Davis summed things up when he remarked, "You've never seen such nuttiness in your life."[72]

The Rat Pack made a few loose-limbed movies together, including *Ocean's 11* and *Robin and the 7 Hoods*. Sinatra's other movies from this period and later included the usual mix of genres: thrillers (*Tony Rome*); comedies (*Marriage on the Rocks*); war dramas (*None but the Brave*); spy pictures (*The Naked Runner*); and Westerns (*Dirty Dingus Magee*). None was as successful as his earlier films; it seemed that Sinatra's creative output in film dropped as the years progressed, that he had lost his knack for picking good scripts.

(Left to right) Peter Lawford, Dean Martin, Sammy Davis Jr., and Sinatra in a still from the Rat Pack movie Ocean's 11.

THROWING BURGERS

In these passages from his biography All Or Nothing at All, *Donald Clarke discusses some of Sinatra's less savory attributes.*

"On the plus side was his instinctive feeling for the underdog; he hated racism, anti-Semitism or injustice of any kind. . . . But his hatred of injustice was in the abstract. When it came to individual underdogs, they were either his friends or his enemies, and woe to them if they stepped out of line; neither strangers nor close friends were immune.

He threw hamburgers at the wall; he sometimes had members of the public beaten up if they had the temerity to approach him for the purpose of hero-worship; on one occasion he punched a bartender at a party because a drink didn't come fast enough. . . . The man who wanted to be the coolest animal who ever walked too often lost his cool [and] the only time he seemed to be in complete control of himself was when he was behind a microphone. . . .

His obsessiveness, his bad temper, and his awful relationships with women were simply clues to the fact that no matter how big a star he was, he could never get enough attention. He was a spoiled brat. . . . Sinatra became a star because he was a great pop singer, and subsequently remained one of the most famous people in the world partly because he could behave badly and get away with it."

While shooting *None but the Brave* in Hawaii in 1964, Sinatra went swimming with a group of friends. The singer and the wife of the film's executive producer were caught in an undertow and swept out to sea; they became exhausted and nearly drowned. Fortunately, a young actor, Brad Dexter, swam to their rescue and kept them alive until more help arrived on surfboards. In gratitude, Sinatra hired Dexter as a producer for his film company.

CONNECTIONS: UNDERWORLD AND POLITICAL

The Rat Pack was not the only social group to which Sinatra belonged. All his life, Sinatra had enjoyed the company of tough guys, the tougher the better; the Mob had moved into Vegas in a big way beginning in the late 1940s, and entertainment was just one aspect of its hold on the city. Thus, anyone who was in the entertainment business

Sinatra (right) sits next to John F. Kennedy at a fund-raiser in Los Angeles in 1960. Kennedy enjoyed spending time with Sinatra as well as the rest of the Rat Pack.

in Las Vegas encountered organized crime figures as a virtual occupational hazard.

Sinatra's underworld connections led to the singer testifying on several occasions before state- and federal-level grand juries investigating organized crime. Although no indictments against him were ever handed down, rumors of associations with organized crime dogged Sinatra all his life; as one observer put it, "Frank Sinatra has been the victim of printer's ink."[73]

One such friendship was with Sam Giancana, the top mobster in Chicago, who called the singer "the Canary." This connection intersected with another set of friends: the powerful Kennedy family of Massachusetts.

In the late 1950s, John F. Kennedy, then a charismatic U.S. senator and a presidential hopeful, was frequently seen with the Rat Pack. Kennedy, whom Sinatra called "Chicky-Boy," loved the Pack, with its glamorous stars and available women, and he fit in perfectly. Peter Lawford told a reporter, "Let's just say that the Kennedys are interested in the lively arts, and that Sinatra is the liveliest art of all."[74]

For his part, Sinatra, always a strong supporter of Democratic politics, reveled in his connection with a powerful politician and worked hard for Kennedy during the campaign of 1960.

After the Rat Pack sang the national anthem at the 1960 Democratic National Convention, when Kennedy was nominated, the singer campaigned hard to raise money for his man. Sinatra was apparently a very persuasive fund-raiser; Milt Ebbins, Peter Lawford's manager, recalls, "Frank snapped his fingers, and people fell into line. He'd get on the phone to somebody and before you knew it he'd be saying, 'Gotcha down for ten thousand,' and that would be the end of it."[75]

WHITE HOUSE RUMORS

Meanwhile, although nothing has ever been proven, rumors connecting Sinatra, Giancana, and Kennedy have repeatedly surfaced over the years.

One such allegation involves JFK's father, Joseph P. Kennedy, a political string-puller whose career included stints as a bootlegger and ambassador to Great Britain. According to this story, the elder Kennedy knew his son's presidential race would depend on a few key states and cities, including Chicago. The Kennedys, through Sinatra, allegedly asked Giancana to help sway Chicago and Giancana agreed, with the understanding that a future Kennedy administration would soft-pedal federal investigations of his businesses.

After the election, however, JFK reneged on the agreement; he instigated instead a major crackdown on organized crime. Giancana was furious; William F. Roemer, who tracked Giancana for years

Sinatra escorts Jacqueline Kennedy at the January 20, 1961, preinauguration gala staged by Sinatra to help pay for John F. Kennedy's presidential campaign.

as an FBI agent, commented that the mobster's regard for Sinatra "took a 180-degree turn for the worse when he found out that Ol' Blue Eyes wielded a lot less influence than he thought he did."[76]

Persistent rumors also link Sinatra, JFK, and Giancana with certain women. According to one story, Sinatra introduced JFK to one of his own girlfriends, Marilyn Monroe, with whom the president conducted a steamy affair that was not made public until years after the deaths of both Monroe and Kennedy.

Sinatra also introduced Judith Campbell (later Judith Campbell Exner) to both Kennedy and Giancana; Exner later claimed to have had simultaneous affairs with the president and the mobster during the Kennedy administration.

Kennedy asked many favors of Sinatra, including having him produce his inaugural festivities. Once in office, however, JFK began to distance himself from Sinatra and any potential political embarrassment.

Nonetheless, Sinatra extensively altered his second house in Rancho Mirage, hoping that it would become the president's West Coast retreat. He added such touches as a banquet room for forty, two cottages for Secret Service agents, and a communications center with a full switchboard. His daughter Nancy later recalled, "He redecorated every part of the house except his own bedroom."[77]

SNUBBED, BUT LOYAL

When Kennedy visited California in March 1962, he stayed not at Sinatra's house but at Bing Crosby's. Apparently the snub was due to the counsel of Kennedy's advisers, who felt that Sinatra's gangland ties were too hot politically.

The joke around Hollywood was that Sinatra should have put up a plaque in the Rancho Mirage house reading "JACK KENNEDY ALMOST SLEPT HERE." Sinatra was crushed, though he remained a Kennedy loyalist.

Kennedy continued to ask favors of Sinatra throughout his term of office as president. One of these was a request in 1962 that the singer make a world tour as a goodwill gesture to other countries under the auspices of the State Department.

Sinatra had just bought his own jet, however, and was more interested in doing something on his own. He decided to arrange instead a series of concerts benefiting children's hospitals. This two-month world tour was the largest humanitarian gesture of Sinatra's career.

Accompanied by a crack sextet of musicians, Sinatra performed a total of thirty concerts in, among other countries, Mexico, Hong Kong, Japan, Israel, Greece, Italy, France, England, and Monaco. While in England, Sinatra made a record called *Great Songs from Great Britain* (all the compositions being by Britons). This proved to be a disappointing album; however, an excellent recording of the Paris show was later released.

The Paris concert represents one of the few times Sinatra recorded with a small group. The singer is in energetic and playful form, and the choice of material is superior. The notoriously cranky Sinatra can even be heard making a corny

Sinatra and his daughter Nancy perform together on TV in 1966.

joke or two: After he sings the phrase "fighting vainly the old *ennui*" in "I Get a Kick Out of You," he dryly remarks, "That's French."

THE KIDS

Tina, the youngest of Sinatra's children, was still a teenager in the early 1960s, but the singer's older children were adults by now. Nancy and Frank Jr. had both chosen to find their own ways in the entertain-

ment world despite the giant shadow cast by their father.

Nancy set out on a singing career of her own, making a dozen singles for Reprise that went nowhere before she recorded a rock-oriented song in 1966. "These Boots Are Made for Walkin'" went to number one and is still considered a cult classic despite (or perhaps because of) Nancy's modest vocal talents.

Frank Jr. studied music formally and also embarked on a career as a singer; in later decades he became his father's musical director. Perhaps his greatest moment of fame, however, was as a crime victim.

Two weeks after John Kennedy was shot in 1963, the younger Sinatra, who had been singing at a club in Lake Tahoe, Nevada, was kidnapped. His father arranged to pay the ransom the kidnappers demanded, $240,000, but when the singer went to the designated pickup point, his son was not there.

Soon after, Frank Jr. was found stumbling along a highway barefoot, and his kidnappers were caught a few days later. The criminals claimed that they had been hired to abduct the younger Sinatra as a publicity stunt to boost his singing career, but their claim proved baseless and they were sentenced to life terms.

Some newspaper journalists suggested that the idea Frank Jr. had tried to pull a publicity stunt was, in fact, the truth. Regarding this, the elder Sinatra (referring to a serious disease) commented to reporters: "This family needs publicity like it needs peritonitis."[78]

Change

For years Sinatra's brand of popular music had reigned supreme: the solo vocalist singing compositions from the golden age of songwriting. But now a rambunctious new form of pop music—rock and roll—was taking over. Rock was the music of the younger generation, and Sinatra was no longer young. The singer made no secret of his feelings about the new music, which he called "the most brutal, ugly, degenerate, vicious form of expression it has been my displeasure to hear." [79]

For a few years, the two musical cultures overlapped and were almost equally popular. When Dean Martin set to work on a new album, he teased his twelve-year-old son Dino, a Beatles fan, by predicting that he would knock Dino's "little pallies" off the charts. A few months later, Martin's song "Everybody Loves Somebody" unseated the Beatles' "A Hard Day's Night" from the number one spot. In 1967—the same year as the Summer of Love and *Sgt. Pepper's Lonely Hearts Club Band*—Martin hosted the number one TV show in America. And within one year, Sinatra's label Reprise had three gold albums: two were Dean Martin records, and the third was Jimi Hendrix's debut album, *Are You Experienced?*

But soon rock would take over completely, and singers like Sinatra would have difficulty even being heard.

Chapter

7 The Last Decades

May you live to be a hundred years old, and may the last voice you hear be mine.

—Frank Sinatra's favorite toast

Sinatra's fan base was primarily the generation that had lived through both the Great Depression and World War II. Then that generation's children came of age in the late 1960s. Where he once had been an idol, Sinatra and his style of ring-a-ding-ding cool suddenly became a running joke to a generation more concerned with free love, antiwar and civil rights protests, drugs, and rock. Journalist Max Rudin writes, "A new generation was flexing its cultural muscles, and to it, the sixties would mean not Vegas and Miami, casual suburban luxury, and postwar success, but civil rights and Vietnam."[80]

Sinatra had flopped when he had recorded novelty pop singles under the guidance of Mitch Miller; he had reaped great rewards when following his own instincts with albums of classic songs created in conjunction with the likes of Stordahl, May, and Riddle.

Nonetheless, in the '60s and '70s the singer tried to roll with the punches, making records that he thought would appeal to younger audiences. The songs were not to his own taste, but he thought they were potential hits.

A BRIEF RETIREMENT

The results were disheartening. Dismayed at the changes in popular music and frustrated by the poor reception of his recent records, Sinatra announced in March 1971 that he was retiring from the entertainment business. As his daughter Nancy writes, "Dad was 55. A good time to pause and think."[81]

His farewell appearance, at a benefit concert for the Motion Picture and Television Relief Fund, was vintage Sinatra-style theater. His final song was the classic "Angel Eyes," and as he sang its final words— "Scuse me while I disappear"—the spotlight on him snapped off, leaving the stage in darkness as he strolled backstage.

Off the road for the first time in decades, Sinatra tried hard to relax. He spent time with friends. He had always loved to paint, and now he spent hours in his home studio. He played with his model trains, an enthusiasm he had picked up from Tommy Dorsey. He even briefly grew a beard.

Sinatra tries his hand as a photographer in 1971, during the singer's brief retirement. Sinatra found such activities unfulfilling and soon decided to resume performing.

But he was restless. According to one story, an event at the White House made him realize he was not ready to retire. The occasion was a reception in honor of Italian prime minister Giulio Andreotti; Sinatra came out of retirement to sing with an orchestra led by Nelson Riddle. The standing ovation led by President Richard Nixon convinced Sinatra that he needed to be back in the spotlight.

Within two years he had returned to regular performance—or, as his public relations firm put it, Ol' Blue Eyes was back. (This phrase was also the title of an album and a TV special.) His home base was, at least temporarily, again the Sands Casino in Las Vegas.

Sinatra's un-retirement turned out to be well timed; the media proved to be even more interested in him than ever. Biogra-

pher Will Friedwald dryly notes, "Sinatra was getting more play in the press than ever before, and he didn't have to punch or marry anybody or even show up before an organized-crime commission."[82]

BAD BOY

Which is not to say that Sinatra dropped his bad-boy image. As many have remarked, even if only half the stories told about the singer were true, he still led a colorful and tempestuous life.

On one occasion, he ran up $200,000 in gambling markers at the Sands Casino and asked for more credit. When Carl Cohen, the casino manager, refused, Sinatra climbed into a baggage cart and steered it into a plate-glass window, then picked a fight with Cohen that resulted in the singer losing the caps on two front teeth.

He stormed out of the Sands and never returned, arranging instead a long-term agreement with Caesar's Palace. Billboards for his performances there did not even need to mention his name, instead reading simply: HE'S HERE!!

As always, much of the gossip about Sinatra revolved around his love life.

In 1966 the singer married for a third time, to an unlikely partner: Mia Farrow, the star of the prime-time TV soap opera *Peyton Place*. The actress was twenty when she married Sinatra—thirty-odd years younger than the singer and five years younger than his oldest child.

Farrow was the daughter of two Hollywood legends, actress Maureen O'Hara and director John Farrow. Her waiflike, wispy demeanor was at striking odds to the rough-hewn Sinatra. Sinatra's friends, and Sinatra watchers around the world, were mystified by the odd union. In the opinion of Mia's mother, the reason had something to do with Sinatra's powerful need to pamper and shelter women: "Men had an instinctive desire to protect Mia. That's the secret."[83]

FROM MIA TO BARBARA

The marriage, in any case, was short-lived. They drifted quickly apart, and the end came when Sinatra insisted Farrow quit her starring role in the horror film *Rosemary's Baby* to join him in the movie he was then shooting, *The Detective*.

The actress refused and Sinatra had divorce papers served on his wife's movie set. When her film finished shooting, Farrow fled the country and traveled to India to join the Beatles in their studies with a fashionable guru, Maharishi Mahesh Yogi. Reflecting later on her failed marriage, she remarked, "It was a little bit like an adoption that I had somehow messed up."[84] For his part, Sinatra commented a dozen years after the end of the marriage, "I still don't know what *that* was all about."[85]

Many girlfriends later, Sinatra married for a fourth time.

Zeppo and Barbara Marx had long been neighbors of Sinatra at his second home in Rancho Mirage. Zeppo Marx was the least-famous member of the Marx Brothers comedy team, and his wife was a

Sinatra and actress Mia Farrow were married in 1966.

former beauty queen and chorus girl. After the Marxes divorced in the early 1970s, Barbara Marx gradually grew closer to Sinatra.

The singer proposed marriage when they were out at dinner one night. Sinatra dropped a seventeen-karat diamond ring in Barbara's champagne glass when her head was turned. She later recalled, "He was going to put it in the soup, he said, but he was afraid I'd eat it. I'd drunk more than half the glass before I saw it. I thought it was an ice cube."[86]

They married in 1976. It would prove to be the longest lasting and most stable of all of Sinatra's relationships, remaining intact until his death. Barbara was willing to acquiesce to her husband's wishes in almost everything. Nonetheless, when asked how they maintained a stable relationship, she joked, "Well, we fight a lot."[87]

After a rocky love life, Sinatra found stability with his fourth wife, Barbara.

HONORS AND CHARITY WORK

In his final decades, Sinatra became more active than before in raising money for charities, performing twelve to fifteen benefit concerts a year. In just five concerts, for instance, he raised more than $9 million for the Memorial Sloan-Kettering Cancer Center. In 1983 he raised money through the Variety Club for a new wing of Children's Orthopedic Hospital in Seattle.

He also began accumulating numerous awards and honors. In 1983 he was awarded the Kennedy Center Award for Lifetime Achievement. In 1984, while in Austria to organize a gala concert raising money for children's charities, he received that country's highest civilian honor, the Medal of Honor for Science and Art.

That same year he was awarded an honorary doctorate from Loyola Marymount University. He had already become the first singer to be heard in outer space: The *Apollo 11* astronauts, the first to land on the moon, brought along a tape of Sinatra singing an obvious choice: "Fly Me to the Moon."

In 1985 the singer received an honorary doctorate in engineering from Stevens Institute of Technology in Hoboken; it was the first time he had returned to Hoboken in over thirty years. That same year he received America's highest civilian honor, the Presidential Medal of Freedom.

The Hoboken trip was in part a campaign stop for Ronald Reagan, then seeking another term as president. Sinatra had produced Reagan's first inaugural gala in 1981 and also performed at Reagan's second inaugural party. Sinatra's politics had taken a conservative turn in his later years, and he publicly supported the Republican Reagan as he had earlier supported another right-wing politician, Richard Nixon.

Yet another honor had been awarded to Sinatra in 1971, when he was awarded the Jean Hersholt Humanitarian Award, an honorary Oscar in recognition of his charity work. In his acceptance speech, Sinatra spoke of how many others deserved it:

> If your name is John Doe, and you work day and night doing things for your helpless neighbors, what you get for your effort is *tired*. So Mr. and Mrs. Doe, and all of you who give of yourselves to those who carry too big a burden to make it on their own, I want you to reach out and take your share of this. . . . Because if I have earned it, so, too, have you.[88]

MIXED RECORDINGS

Beginning in the late 1960s and continuing into the early '80s, Sinatra recorded material that he hoped would catch public fashions.

One song, written by Paul Anka and recorded in 1968, came to be closely associated with Sinatra and his macho image. "My Way" is not a brilliant piece of music, and Sinatra eventually came to dislike it intensely; nonetheless, his interpretation of the song—with its bold assertion that "I did it my way"—made for great theater. Will Friedwald comments that the singer's performance "had the desired effect of making the song both a summation of and a metaphor for Sinatra's entire career."[89]

Sinatra accepts an award from Hebrew University in Israel in 1978.

Nearly everything else Sinatra recorded during this period, however, was an artistic disappointment. There were good individual songs on almost all of his records, but no single album was a complete success. Not only did he choose inferior folk rock and soft rock material, poorly suited to his style and persona; he also worked with producers and arrangers who were not up to the standards of his best collaborators.

Furthermore, the records were disappointing financially. Sinatra did score a few hit singles, like "Strangers in the Night," his first number one recording since 1955. Another hit was a duet with his daughter Nancy, "Somethin' Stupid"; more than one wag has suggested, however, that Sinatra's other recordings of this period ought to have been called "Somethin' Even More Stupid."

In the Studio

Producer Jimmy Bowen worked with Sinatra in the singer's later years, when they were trying to create hit records with soft rock material. In these excerpts from Friedwald's Sinatra: The Song Is You: A Singer's Art, *he recalls how Sinatra sometimes needed to be challenged during recording sessions.*

"When we finished cutting 'Softly (As I Leave You)' we were listening to the playbacks and Frank said, 'Well, James, what do you think?' And I said, 'I think it's [only] about a number thirty record, but it'll get us back on radio.' He looked at me like that didn't please him too much, and he left. And I think the record went to twenty-seven or twenty-eight. But with Sinatra that would be important because your word is very important to him, and that's what I felt. . . .

[On another occasion] Sinatra arrived, went to work, and soon came up with a performance of 'That's Life' that almost all present were sure was 'the one.' We played it back, and Frank said, 'Boy! That's a hit, isn't it!' And I said, 'Well, no. If you want a hit, you're going to have to do it one more time.' Everybody got real quiet, and he gave me the coldest look an artist ever gave me. But he went right out, and instead of singing it hip—he was pissed now—he bit it! That's when he sang 'That's Life'!"

One particularly low point came with the 1970 album *Watertown*. The concept was a good one for Sinatra—a song cycle about a middle-aged, small-town man whose wife is leaving him. Unfortunately, Sinatra chose as his songwriter Bob Gaudio, who had composed hits for the Four Seasons but whose style was wildly unsuited to the older singer. The album did not even make the top one hundred chart.

In 1977 Sinatra even tried his hand at disco, and in 1980 hit another low point with the three-record album *Trilogy: Past, Present, and Future.* This was another con-cept album, this time put together by producer Sonny Burke. The first album, *Past*, was a pleasant recreation of Sinatra's old hits, arranged and conducted by Billy May. *Present* was yet another set of mediocre soft rock. *Future*, meanwhile, was a strange suite of songs composed, arranged, and conducted by Gordon Jenkins. Backed by the Los Angeles Philharmonic, alto and soprano soloists, and a large chorus, Sinatra sang lyrics concerning such topics as space travel, world peace, and living in the desert.

Sinatra did record some good material during his last decades. He made a pleasant album with the Brazilian bossa nova guitarist Antonio Carlos Jobim, the composer of "The Girl from Ipanema." Another good record, *September of My Years*, was a bittersweet concept album with Gordon Jenkins that found Sinatra playing the role of a man looking back with amusement and regret at his life; its strong selection of material includes two songs now closely associated with Sinatra, "It Was a Very Good Year" and "September Song."

DUETS

By the '90s, all that might be reasonably expected of Sinatra would be a few farewell appearances and a retreat from public life. Instead, the singer pulled a surprise: In 1993, in his late seventies and after a decade of no new records, he released the album *Duets*.

It was a reversal of his past attempts at confronting the rock generation: instead of recording rock songs, Sinatra turned the concept around by recording a collection of classic American songbook tunes with such contemporary singers as Bono, Aretha Franklin, and Bruce Springsteen.

Working with prominent rock producer Phil Ramone, Sinatra recorded his vocals live with an orchestra, with the contributions of the other singers overdubbed later. (This practice of overdubbing duets was hardly new; it dates back at least to 1948, when Doris Day and Buddy Clark recorded their hit "My Darling, My Darling" in three sessions, one for the band and one for each singer.)

The sessions were beset with problems. Sinatra questioned the wisdom of re-recording songs he'd done many times before. Ramone and his engineer, meanwhile, had to alter Sinatra's vocals after he recorded them, changing them slightly to correct his sometimes faltering intonation and pitch.

Despite the production difficulties, the public loved the results. The album reached number two on the *Billboard* chart and became the biggest-selling recording

Aretha Franklin, one of the contributors to Sinatra's 1993 album Duets.

In Will Friedwald's Sinatra: The Song Is You: A Singer's Art, *Frank Foster, who often shared the stage with Sinatra in his role as saxophonist for (and later leader of) the Count Basie Orchestra, reflects on Sinatra's performances in his later years.*

"After all these years, his voice is going, and at seventy-eight what do you expect? But he still has the same charisma, the same ability to stir a crowd that he had years ago. It may seem like a shame that they have to have four monitors on stage to flash the lyrics in front of him and that he makes heavy use of them. Hey, man, if you're still going professionally at seventy-eight, it's no disgrace to use whatever props are necessary, especially when you can still fill Radio City Music Hall for an entire week."

of the singer's career. Its success prompted a sequel in 1994, *Duets II*, with an equally diverse cast of guests including Stevie Wonder, Chrissie Hynde, and Willie Nelson.

Sinatra purists hated the *Duets* albums, calling them still more crass attempts to attract a younger audience. In the opinion of Will Friedwald, the concept of having rock singers interpret tunes from Sinatra's era was ludicrous: "It's as if the Yankees were to hire Cindy Crawford to pitch naked; she would certainly bring in crowds, but she can't play the game."[90]

THE FINAL TOURS

Sinatra continued to tour regularly until close to the end of his life. Unlike the easy-going Rat Pack years, however, he sang now in huge theaters and stadiums, a situation ill-suited to his intimate style, and each show took on the aspect of a big event. What was lost in intimacy during these final years was made up for in audience numbers; it has been estimated that more people saw Sinatra live in the last two decades of his life than in the rest of his career put together.

An attempt to reunite the Rat Pack for a tour in 1988 nearly fell apart after one week; Dean Martin, severely depressed since his jet pilot son's death in a plane crash, abruptly left the tour. He was replaced by Liza Minelli, the daughter of longtime Sinatra friend Judy Garland.

Many of Sinatra's close friends and associates, meanwhile, were falling by the wayside. In the 1980s Gordon Jenkins, Nelson Riddle, drummer Buddy Rich (an old friend from the Dorsey days), and Sinatra's longtime drummer Irv Cottler all passed away. In 1990 Sammy Davis Jr. died, followed within a few years by such Sinatra intimates as songwriters Jule Styne, Jimmy

Van Heusen, and Sammy Cahn; agent Swifty Lazar; and Sinatra's longtime friend and bodyguard Jilly Rizzo. Both his parents were dead, and in 1995 Dean Martin also passed away.

Despite an iron constitution, Sinatra was also showing unmistakable signs of aging; he was no longer the rail-thin "boy singer" or the swinging Rat Packer. His body was thickening. He had undergone emergency surgery for diverticulitis. He had lost his already thinning hair; according to legend, he hired a woman whose only job was to care for his forty toupees. He quit smoking cigarettes and rarely drank; his daughter Tina joked, "He's more conscious of mortality. He's calmed down. In fact, he's gotten quite dull."[91]

His eyesight was failing, his onstage patter was sometimes rambling and incoherent, and he experienced occasional memory problems; he needed TelePrompTers to feed him lyrics that he'd sung for forty years. Sinatra's pianist Bill Miller commented about such lapses, "He'd apologize to the audience. They'd say, 'Hey, Frank, we don't care.' And they don't. They want to see *him*."[92]

AGING

Sinatra's voice, meanwhile, was becoming deeper and coarser. He was unable to hit the notes and achieve the once-bottomless depths of emotion that he once could, although he still had his famous phrasing, his powerful personality was still present, and the famous blue eyes were as intense as ever. Typical of the critical reaction to the aging Sinatra was this comment from the Sydney *Daily Mirror* during a 1974 tour:

> Too much booze, too many smokes, too many long, long nights have taken the glow from his voice, but no one gave a damn. . . . For Sinatra still has the phrasing which cannot be surpassed,

Though Sinatra's abilities diminished somewhat with age, audiences nonetheless loved seeing him perform.

ANOMALIES

Frank Sinatra Jr. was one of the most stirring speakers at his father's memorial service. He is quoted in Christina Cheakalos's 1998 article in People Weekly, *"So Long, Sinatra."*

"My father's whole life was an anomaly. His birth was so difficult that the fact that he lived at all was an anomaly. That he even became a singer, that he became a great singer and that he made such wonderful movies, all this was an anomaly. . . . And how did he live to such a ripe old age, which was certainly not because he took care of himself? That's the greatest anomaly."

Sinatra and his son Frank, Jr., in 1963.

the timing, the splendid arrogance of remarkable talent.[93]

His onstage patter had always been a stream-of-consciousness ramble, but now it began to wander even more than it had and sometimes became incoherent. At the 1994 Grammy Awards, Sinatra appeared on television to accept a Lifetime Achievement Award. However, Sinatra's acceptance speech was crudely cut off by a commercial because the show's producers worried that he might begin rambling.

A few days later the singer, tired and overheated, briefly collapsed onstage in Richmond, Virginia. But he waved gamely to the audience as he was carried off, the audience giving him a standing ovation, and two weeks later he was back on the road.

In 1995 Sinatra sold the luxurious desert estate he had owned since 1954—a compound that included a helipad, a swimming pool, tennis courts, a screening room, and twenty-four-hour kitchen service. He and Barbara moved permanently to their Beverly Hills home and auctioned off many of their possessions.

He also arranged his will to guarantee that his large fortune would be distributed his way. After his death, the will stated, any family member who contested its contents would be automatically disinherited. Sinatra arranged for several large bequests; for example, the Malibu beach house, the Beverly Hills mansion, and up to $3.5 million went to Barbara Sinatra; $200,000 each and undivided interest in a luxurious Beverly Hills office building were for his children, who already shared the rights to most of his lucrative music catalog (Frank Jr. received sole rights to his father's sheet music); and $1 million went to his two granddaughters.

The year 1995, which saw several gala celebrations in honor of the singer's eightieth birthday, was also the year of Sinatra's last public performance. In February he sang six songs for a private audience on the last day of the Frank Sinatra Desert Classic golf tournament. After that, he and Barbara led a very quiet life in Los Angeles.

THE END

Frank Sinatra died of a heart attack on May 14, 1998. He was eighty-two. As might be expected, the news made headlines around the world, and tributes poured in from singers, musicians, film stars, politicians, and ordinary fans everywhere.

The memorial service on May 20 was held at Good Shepherd Catholic Church in Beverly Hills. Over a thousand onlookers and a hundred photographers stood outside; seven hundred guests crowded inside, including his children, his widow, and two of his ex-wives. Ava Gardner had died in 1990.

The mourners sat among thirty thousand white roses, gardenias, and chrysanthemums, listening to Sinatra tunes played by pianist Bill Miller. Archbishop Roger Mahony of Los Angeles officiated, and among those offering eulogies were Joey Bishop and actors Gregory Peck, Kirk Douglas, and Robert Wagner. Frank Jr. was the last speaker at the two-hour affair, ending his eulogy with the words his father had spoken at Harry James's funeral in 1983: "Thanks for everything. So long, buddy, and take care of yourself."[94]

But it was Sinatra himself who closed the show, with a recording of "Put Your Dreams Away" serenading the crowd. Actor Ben Vereen commented on Sinatra getting in the final word: "You could hear everyone gasp. . . . It was like he rose up on the edge of the coffin; like he was saying, 'Hey, Charlie, check this out!'"[95]

The Chairman of the Board was buried close to his parents at Desert Memorial Park in Cathedral City, near Palm Springs. Like an ancient king, he was buried with a variety of precious items: accompanying him into the grave were a bottle of Jack Daniel's whiskey, a Zippo lighter, a pack of Camel cigarettes, and ten dimes—the latter because Sinatra always hated the idea of being stranded someplace where he could not make a phone call.

■

An American Icon

We will still be confronted with Frank's presence in so many ways. I don't know anybody who has influenced so many musicians and will continue to do so.

—songwriter/singer Paul Anka

Frank Sinatra has, without a doubt, left a lasting legacy in American popular music.

Perhaps most importantly, Sinatra's unparalleled way with the classic American songbook has been a continuing influence on younger popular singers. One of the best and best-known of these is Sinatra's friend and fellow "saloon singer" Tony Bennett.

Ten years younger than Sinatra, Bennett has become a favorite with an even younger generation than his own. Unlike Sinatra's unsuccessful efforts late in life to reach a younger audience, Bennett never changed his choice of material. Instead, he continued to sing in his own style until the younger generation was ready to hear him. Bennett has always readily acknowledged the importance of Sinatra in his own musical education; one of his best albums is *Perfectly Frank*, a tribute to his mentor.

Other singers and musicians have paid similar tribute, including some not associated with Sinatra-era singing. Ringo Starr and Carly Simon are only two of the many rock singers who have recorded albums of standards that are at least indirectly influenced by Sinatra. Linda Ronstadt convinced Nelson Riddle to come out of retirement to help her with three albums of standards that are clear tributes to the singer.

The fad for so-called cocktail music in the 1990s gave Sinatra's ring-a-ding-ding style of cool a boost among young music fans. Writer Max Rudin has commented that this trend seemed to be a reaction to the difficulties of modern life:

> There's irony in the fact that the Rat Pack, like the cocktail and the cigar, has lately been taken up as an emblem of a new political incorrectness. The drinking, the smoking, the swinging insouciance [nonchalance] seem like a vacation from the economic and political pressures of nineties America.[96]

Modern-day tributes to Sinatra have not been necessarily limited to music. For instance, director Steven Soderburgh is planning a remake of the quintessential Rat Pack movie, *Ocean's 11*, with George Clooney reprising the Sinatra role.

A Wider Influence

Besides the strictly musical, Sinatra has had a far wider influence, on his audience as well as his fellow musicians. His campaigning for equality and respect among racial and ethnic groups both presaged and was contemporary with the civil rights era. His embodiment of the immigrant dream—the Italian kid from the street who makes good—has been an inspiration to many.

(At the same time, his famously ill temper and penchant for violence and violent friends were undoubtedly negative influences as well.)

On a more personal level, Sinatra's unparalleled combination of strength and gentleness, letting tenderness mingle with manliness in his persona, served as a role model for countless males of his generation. Pete Hamill writes:

> [He] perfected the role of the Tender Tough Guy and passed it on to several generations of Americans. Before him, the archetype did not exist in American popular culture. That is one reason why he continues to matter; Frank

---

THE NEXT GENERATION

Sinatra has by now influenced several generations of singers. Quoted in Whitney Balliett's book American Singers: 27 Portraits in Song, *the distinguished songwriter and music critic Alec Wilder has this to say about Tony Bennett, the best-known of Sinatra's "children."*

"The list of 'believers' isn't very long. But those who are on it are very special people. Among them, certainly, is Tony Bennett. But first I should say what I mean by a believer. He is one whose sights stay high, who makes as few concessions as he can, whose ideals will not permit him to follow false trails or fashions for notoriety's or security's sake, who takes chances, who seeks to convey, by whatever means, his affections and convictions, and who has faith in the power of beauty to survive, no matter how much squalor and ugliness seek to suppress it. . . . There is a quality about [Bennett's singing] that lets you in. Frank Sinatra's singing mesmerizes you. In fact, it gets so symbolic sometimes that you can't make the relationship with him as a man, even though you may know him. Bennett's professionalism doesn't block you off. It even suggests that maybe you'll see him later at the beer parlor."

Frank Sinatra's songs formed a vital component of American popular music and continue to delight listeners today.

Sinatra created a new model for American masculinity.[97]

Sinatra's presence as an American icon is still strongly felt. There are dozens of Internet websites devoted to him, ranging from the official family site to heartfelt sites produced by fans. His name and his voice are synonymous around the world with romance and swinging good times. His music and legacy have even reached academia; in 1998 Hofstra University sponsored a conference on Sinatra that included such distinguished guests as Quincy Jones.

A number of books about Sinatra were published near the end of his life. They range in quality from Kitty Kelley's notorious tell-all *His Way* (the publication of which Sinatra unsuccessfully tried to stop) to more credible volumes like *Sinatra: The Song Is You: A Singer's Art* by music historian Will Friedwald and *Sinatra: The Artist and the Man* by the *New Yorker's* theater critic John Lahr.

Books about Sinatra continue to appear even after his death. His albums, all re-released on CD, continue to sell well. New Sinatra material, such as concert recordings and radio broadcasts, periodically appear as well. For the singer's family and fans, it seems that—as Sinatra himself memorably sang—the best is yet to come.

Notes

Introduction

1. Quoted in Francis Davis, "Missing from Much of the Recent Commentary on Frank Sinatra, Oddly, Was One Pertinent Topic: What He Meant for Music," *Atlantic Monthly,* Sept. 1, 1998, pp. 120ff.

2. Pete Hamill, *Why Sinatra Matters.* Boston: Little, Brown, 1998, pp. 93–94.

3. Whitney Balliett, *American Singers: 27 Portraits in Song.* New York: Oxford University Press, 1988, p. 132.

4. Quoted in Nancy Sinatra, *Frank Sinatra: An American Legend.* Santa Monica, CA: General Publishing Group, 1995, p. 265.

5. Donald Clarke, *All or Nothing at All: A Life of Frank Sinatra.* New York: Fromm International, 1997, pp. xii–xiii.

Chapter 1: Escaping Hoboken

6. Quoted in Nancy Sinatra, *Frank Sinatra: My Father.* New York: Doubleday, 1985, p. 42.

7. Clarke, *All or Nothing at All,* p. 251.

8. Quoted in Hamill, *Why Sinatra Matters,* p. 84.

9. Quoted in Hamill, *Why Sinatra Matters,* p. 70.

10. Quoted in Hamill, *Why Sinatra Matters,* p. 53.

11. Quoted in John Lahr, *Sinatra: The Artist and the Man.* New York: Random House, 1997, p. 7.

12. Quoted in Lahr, *Sinatra,* p. 9.

13. Quoted in Hamill, *Why Sinatra Matters,* p. 100.

14. Quoted in Clarke, *All or Nothing at All,* p. 18.

15. Hamill, *Why Sinatra Matters,* p. 102.

16. Quoted in Lahr, *Sinatra,* p. 11.

17. Quoted in Sinatra, *Frank Sinatra: My Father,* p. 49.

Chapter 2: On the Road with Harry and Tommy

18. Quoted in Will Friedwald, *Sinatra: The Song Is You: A Singer's Art.* New York: Scribner, 1995, p. 67.

19. Quoted in Hamill, *Why Sinatra Matters,* p. 71.

20. Quoted in Friedwald, *Sinatra,* p. 69.

21. Quoted in Hamill, *Why Sinatra Matters,* p. 105.

22. Quoted in Clarke, *All or Nothing at All,* p. 35.

23. Quoted in Shawn Levy, *Rat Pack Confidential: Frank, Dean, Sammy, Peter, Joey, and the Last Great Showbiz Party.* New York: Doubleday, 1998, p. 24.

24. Quoted in Gene Lees, *Singers and the Song.* New York: Oxford University Press, 1987, p. 104.

25. Quoted in Friedwald, *Sinatra,* p. 24.

26. Quoted in Friedwald, *Sinatra,* p. 86.

27. Quoted in Sinatra, *Frank Sinatra: My Father,* p. 59.

28. Quoted in Clarke, *All or Nothing at All,* p. 56.

29. Quoted in Clarke, *All or Nothing at All,* p. 65.

Chapter 3: Swoonatra!

30. Quoted in Friedwald, *Sinatra,* p. 124.

31. Lahr, *Sinatra,* p. 40.

32. Quoted in Lahr, *Sinatra,* p. 14.

33. Quoted in Sinatra, *Frank Sinatra: An American Legend,* p. 55.

34. Quoted in Sinatra, *Frank Sinatra: My Father,* p. 83.

35. Quoted in Friedwald, *Sinatra*, p. 137.

36. Quoted in Lahr, *Sinatra*, p. 62.

37. Quoted in Friedwald, *Sinatra*, p. 166.

38. Quoted in Hamill, *Why Sinatra Matters*, p. 137.

39. Quoted in Sinatra, *Frank Sinatra: My Father*, p. 95.

40. Robert Horton, "One Good Take: Sinatra, 1915–1998," *Film Comment*, July–August 1998, pp. 14ff.

41. Quoted in Levy, *Rat Pack Confidential*, p. 68.

42. Quoted in Jerry Adler, "Something About Frank," *Newsweek*, Dec. 21, 1998, p. 58.

43. Quoted in Levy, *Rat Pack Confidential*, p. 129.

Chapter 4: Down and Up Again

44. Quoted in Bill Zehme, *The Way You Wear Your Hat: Frank Sinatra and the Lost Art of Livin'*. New York: HarperCollins, 1997, p. 206.

45. Clarke, *All or Nothing at All*, p. 96.

46. Quoted in Clarke, *All or Nothing at All*, p. 97.

47. Quoted in Zehme, *The Way You Wear Your Hat*, p. 144.

48. Quoted in Lahr, *Sinatra*, p. 48.

49. Quoted in Lahr, *Sinatra*, p. 51.

50. Clarke, *All or Nothing at All*, p. 121.

51. Quoted in Lahr, *Sinatra*, p. 53.

52. Quoted in Hamill, *Why Sinatra Matters*, pp. 159–60.

53. Quoted in Clarke, *All or Nothing at All*, p. 123.

54. Quoted in Sinatra, *Frank Sinatra: An American Legend*, p. 106.

Chapter 5: The Classic Years

55. Clarke, *All or Nothing at All*, p. 127.

56. Quoted in Zehme, *The Way You Wear Your Hat*, p. 228.

57. Hamill, *Why Sinatra Matters*, p. 170.

58. Quoted in Friedwald, *Sinatra*, p. 224.

59. Hamill, *Why Sinatra Matters*, p. 177.

60. Quoted in Sinatra, *Frank Sinatra: An American Legend*, p. 141.

61. Hamill, *Why Sinatra Matters*, p. 69.

62. Friedwald, *Sinatra*, p. 249.

63. Quoted in Friedwald, *Sinatra*, p. 367.

64. Quoted in Friedwald, *Sinatra*, p. 368.

65. Quoted in Friedwald, *Sinatra*, p. 415.

66. Quoted in Clarke, *All or Nothing at All*, pp. 148–49.

Chapter 6: The Chairman of the Board

67. Quoted in Zehme, *The Way You Wear Your Hat*, p. 45.

68. Quoted in Zehme, *The Way You Wear Your Hat*, p. 158.

69. Quoted in Sinatra, *Frank Sinatra: My Father*, p. 32.

70. Quoted in Sinatra, *Frank Sinatra: An American Legend*, p. 145.

71. Levy, *Rat Pack Confidential*, p. 101.

72. Quoted in Sinatra, *Frank Sinatra: My Father*, p. 155.

73. Quoted in Sinatra, *Frank Sinatra: My Father*, p. 235.

74. Quoted in Levy, *Rat Pack Confidential*, p. 72.

75. Quoted in Levy, *Rat Pack Confidential*, p. 154.

76. William F. Roemer Jr., *Roemer: Man Against the Mob*. New York: Donald F. Fine, 1989, p. 189.

77. Quoted in Levy, *Rat Pack Confidential*, p. 214.

78. Quoted in Clarke, *All or Nothing at All*, p. 193.

79. Quoted in Bruce Handy, "Frank Sinatra (Time 100: Artists & Entertainers)," *Time*, June 8, 1998, pp. 177ff.

Chapter 7: The Last Decades

80. Max Rudin, "Fly Me to the Moon (Legendary Rat Pack of Entertainment)," *American Heritage*, Dec. 1998, pp. 52ff.

81. Sinatra, *Frank Sinatra: An American Legend*, p. 219.
82. Friedwald, *Sinatra*, p. 459.
83. Quoted in Levy, *Rat Pack Confidential*, p. 271.
84. Quoted in Levy, *Rat Pack Confidential*, p. 272.
85. Quoted in Hamill, *Why Sinatra Matters*, p. 179.
86. Quoted in Zehme, *The Way You Wear Your Hat*, p. 178.
87. Quoted in Zehme, *The Way You Wear Your Hat*, p. 180.
88. Quoted in Sinatra, *Frank Sinatra: My Father*, p. 228.
89. Friedwald, *Sinatra*, p. 447.
90. Friedwald, *Sinatra*, p. 509.
91. Quoted in Sinatra, *Frank Sinatra: My Father*, p. 277.
92. Quoted in Lahr, *Sinatra*, p. 82.
93. Quoted in Clarke, *All or Nothing at All*, p. 240.
94. Quoted in Christina Cheakalos, "So Long, Sinatra," *People Weekly*, June 8, 1998, pp. 58ff.
95. Quoted in Cheakalos, "So Long, Sinatra," p. 58.

Epilogue

96. Rudin, "Fly Me to the Moon,"p. 52.
97. Hamill, *Why Sinatra Matters*, p. 96.

For Further Reading

Lew Irwin, *Sinatra: The Pictorial Biography*. Philadelphia: Courage Books, 1995. This book's minimal text is full of inconsistencies, but it reproduces some terrific early photographs. Not written specifically for young adults.

Nancy Sinatra, *Frank Sinatra: My Father*. New York: Doubleday, 1985. Not written specifically for young adults, this is an understandably generous portrait of the singer by his oldest child, with terrific photos.

———, *Frank Sinatra: An American Legend*. Santa Monica, CA: General Publishing Group, 1995. Not written specifically for young adults, but notable for its candid photos and other memorabilia, scrupulous chronological history, and a CD of music and talk.

Works Consulted

Books

Whitney Balliett, *American Singers: 27 Portraits in Song*. New York: Oxford University Press, 1988. These essays by the jazz critic for the *New Yorker* include multiple references to Sinatra, though no one essay is devoted to him.

Donald Clarke, *All or Nothing at All: A Life of Frank Sinatra*. New York: Fromm International, 1997. Written by the author of a biography of Billie Holiday, this book focuses heavily on Sinatra's recorded output.

Will Friedwald, *Sinatra: The Song Is You: A Singer's Art*. New York: Scribner, 1995. Friedwald is a scholar of American popular music and a steadfast Sinatra fan; this is a super-detailed musical analysis of all his work, incorporating comments from many of Sinatra's musical associates.

Pete Hamill, *Why Sinatra Matters*. Boston: Little, Brown, 1998. This slim book, by a veteran journalist and columnist who was a friend of the singer, is a heartfelt meditation on Sinatra and what he meant to America.

Kitty Kelley, *His Way: The Unauthorized Biography of Frank Sinatra*. New York: Bantam Books, 1986. One of the most notorious of all tell-all biographies, whose publication Sinatra tried to stop. Trashy and mean, with page after page of reconstructed dialogue and other unreliable information.

John Lahr, *Sinatra: The Artist and the Man*. New York: Random House, 1997. Not a full biography, but a long and perceptive critical essay by the drama critic for the *New Yorker*, with many pages of revealing photos.

Gene Lees, *Singers and the Song*. New York: Oxford University Press, 1987. Essays by a distinguished jazz critic, including one on Sinatra.

Shawn Levy, *Rat Pack Confidential: Frank, Dean, Sammy, Peter, Joey, and the Last Great Showbiz Party*. New York: Doubleday, 1998. This chatty book concentrates on the Rat Pack era of Sinatra's life, though it covers other years briefly.

Steven Petkov and Leonard Mustazza, eds., *The Frank Sinatra Reader*. New York: Oxford University Press, 1995. An invaluable source of material from many voices, journalistic and otherwise, spanning all periods of Sinatra's career.

William F. Roemer Jr., *Roemer: Man Against the Mob*. New York: Donald F. Fine, 1989. Contains a section on the alleged connections between Sinatra, John F. Kennedy, and mobster Sam Giancana.

Bill Zehme, *The Way You Wear Your Hat: Frank Sinatra and the Lost Art of Livin'*. New York: HarperCollins, 1997. A strange assortment of sentiment promoting Sinatra's behavior as a paradigm of manly behavior, but an excellent source of firsthand quotes and poignant photos.

Sidney Zion, *Loyalty and Betrayal: The Story of the American Mob*. San Francisco: Collins, 1994. Contains a section on the alleged connections between Sinatra, John F. Kennedy, and mobster Sam Giancana.

Periodicals

Jerry Adler, "Something About Frank," *Newsweek*, Dec. 21, 1998, p. 58.

Christina Cheakalos, "So Long, Sinatra," *People Weekly*, June 8, 1998, pp. 58ff.

Francis Davis, "Missing from Much of the Recent Commentary on Frank Sinatra, Oddly, Was One Pertinent Topic: What He Meant for Music," *Atlantic Monthly*, Sept. 1, 1998, pp. 120ff.

Sammy Davis Jr., "The Frank Sinatra I Know," originally published in *Down Beat*, Aug. 22, 1956, reprinted in *Down Beat*, Aug. 1998, pp. 26ff.

Bruce Handy, "Frank Sinatra (Time 100: Artists & Entertainers)," *Time*, June 8, 1998, pp. 177ff.

Robert Horton, "One Good Take: Sinatra, 1915–1998," *Film Comment*, July–August 1998, pp. 14ff.

Max Rudin, "Fly Me to the Moon (Legendary Rat Pack of Entertainment)," *American Heritage*, Dec. 1998, pp. 52ff.

Index

Picture Credits

On cover: © Marianna Diamos 1978/FPG

© Bettmann/Corbis, 17, 19, 24, 41, 42, 46, 47, 50, 66, 68, 75, 78, 79, 81, 84, 91

Brown Brothers, 16, 27, 31, 60, 61, 67

© Marianna Diamos 1978/FPG, 14

© FPG 1999, 12

FPG, 71

© Robert Maass/Corbis, 89

Photofest, 11, 22, 23, 28, 29, 33, 36, 37, 38, 39, 43, 49, 51, 53, 54, 57, 63, 72, 73, 76, 85, 86, 92, 96

© David Rubinger/Corbis, 87

About the Author

Adam Woog, the author of many books for adults and young adults, has a special interest in twentieth-century American history, popular culture, and biography. He was born on the exact opening day of *From Here to Eternity*, the film that marked Frank Sinatra's comeback from obscurity. Woog lives with his wife and young daughter in his hometown of Seattle, Washington.